This book belongs to:

_____

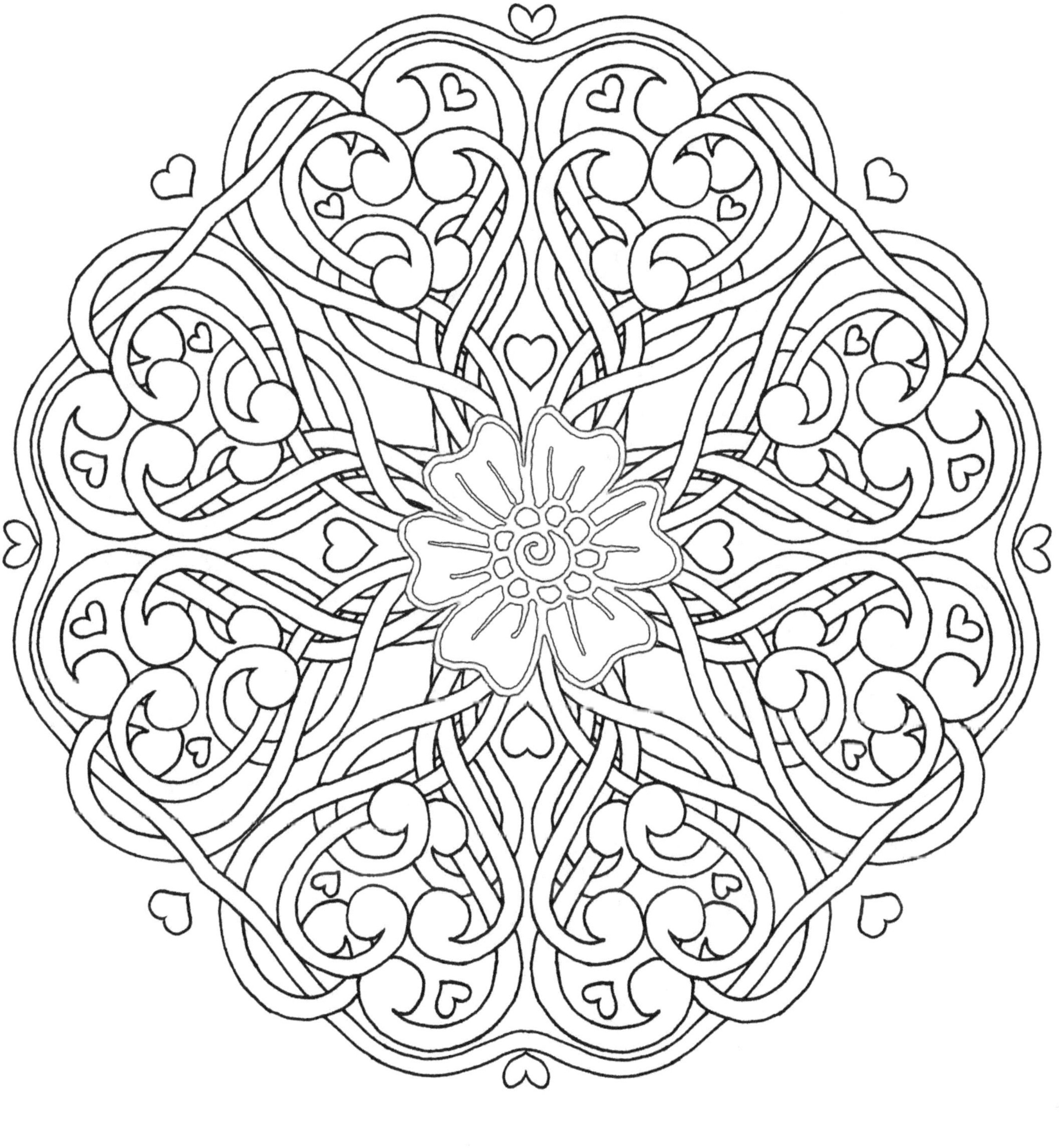

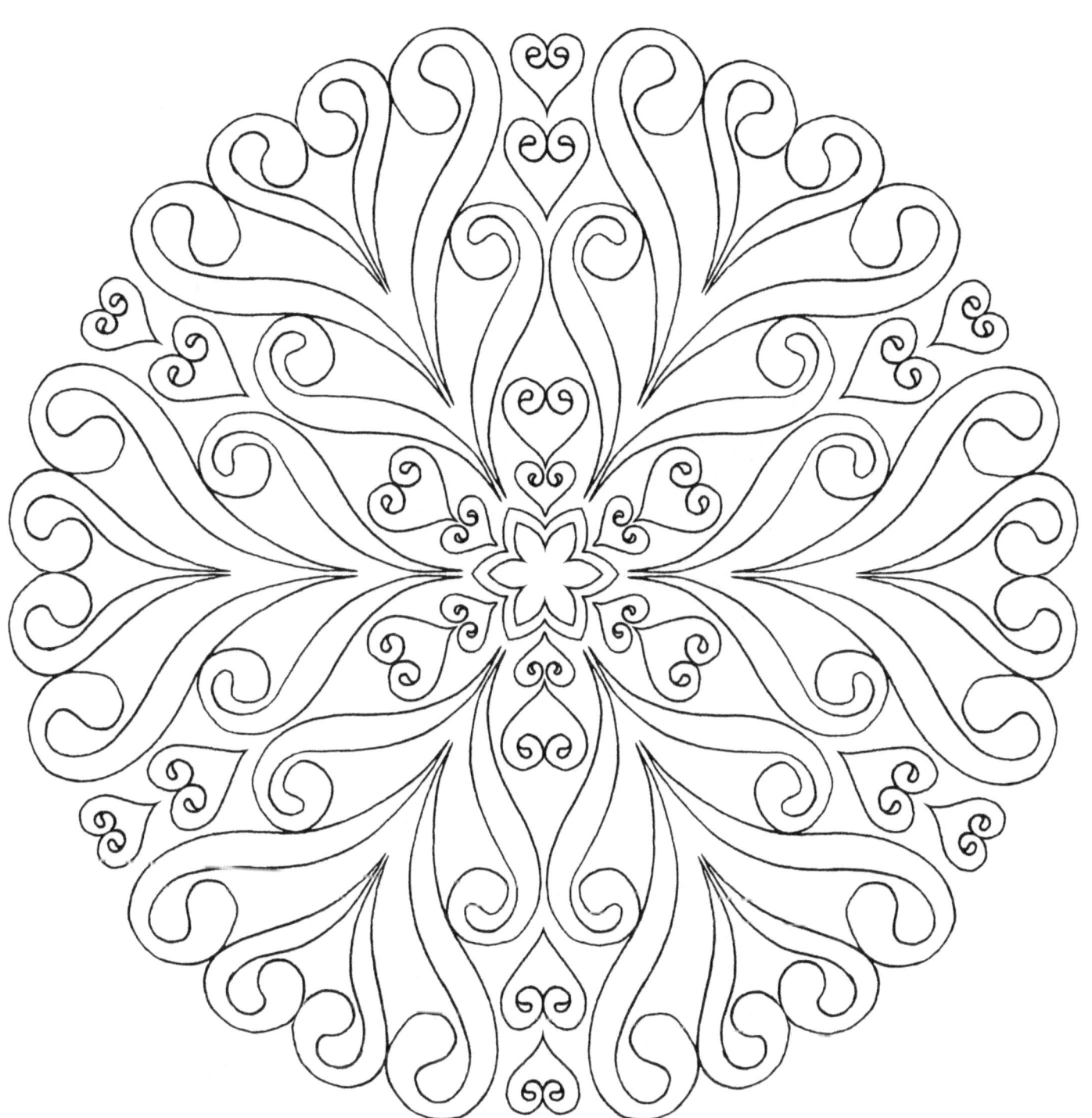

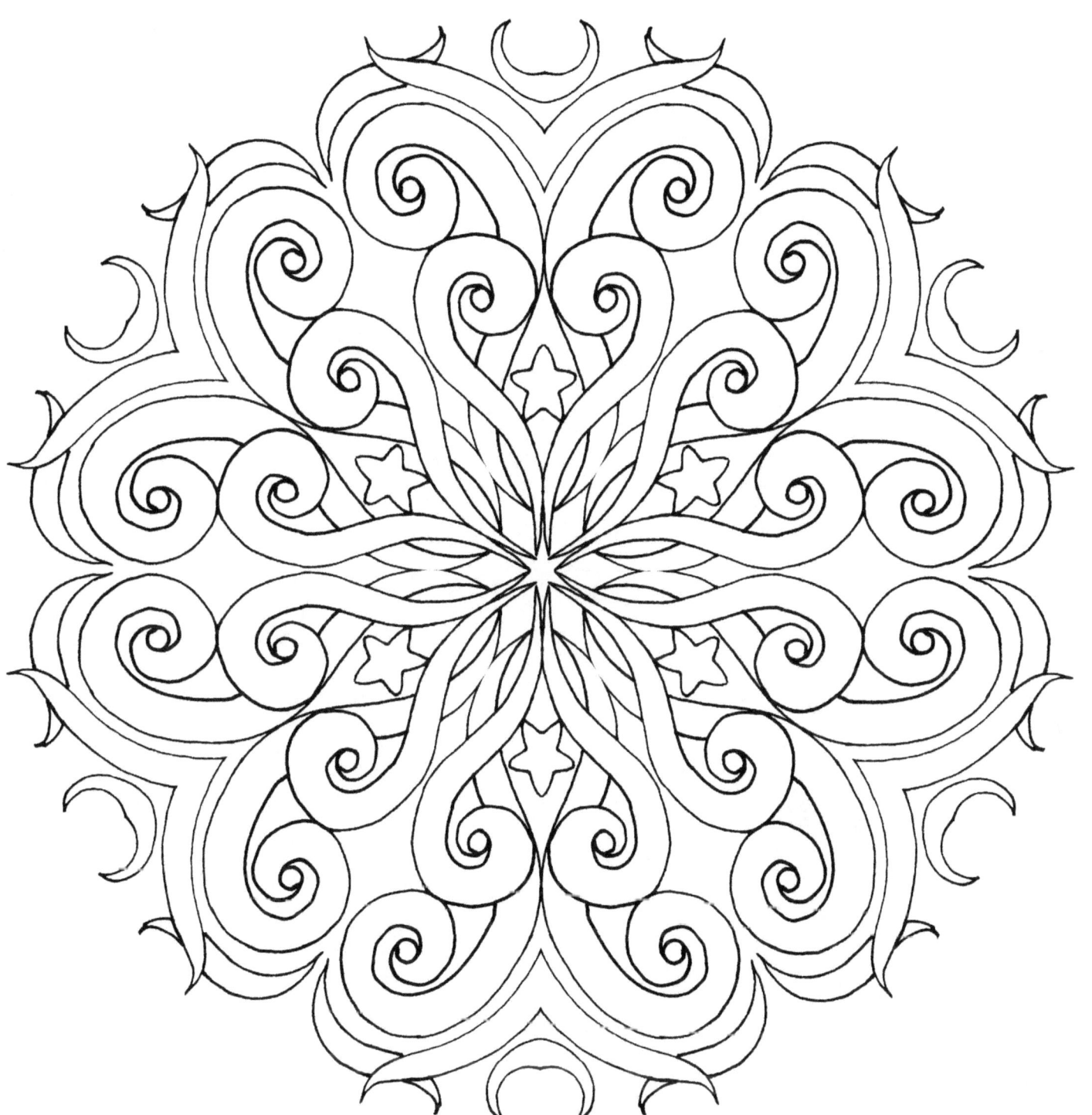

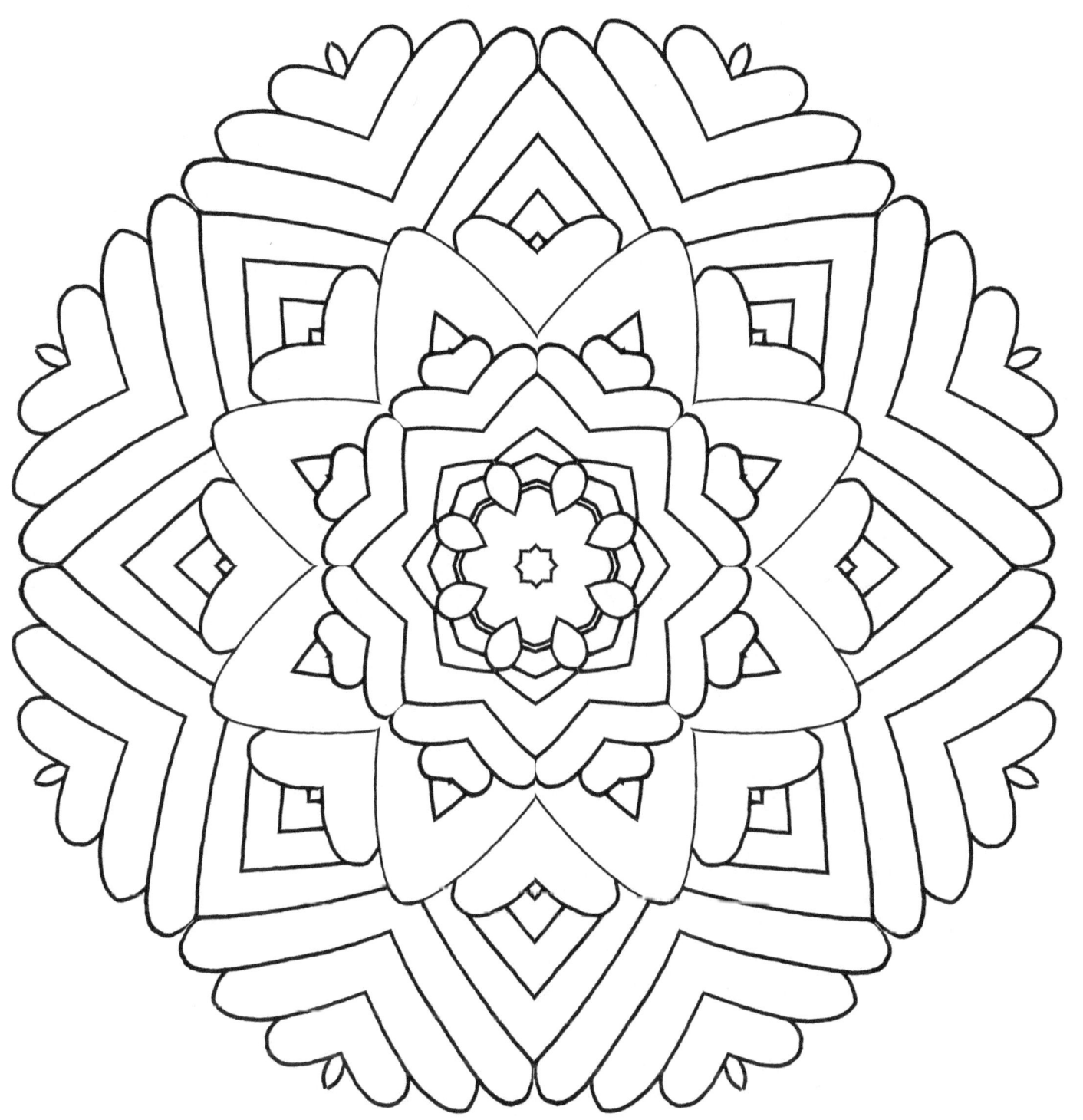

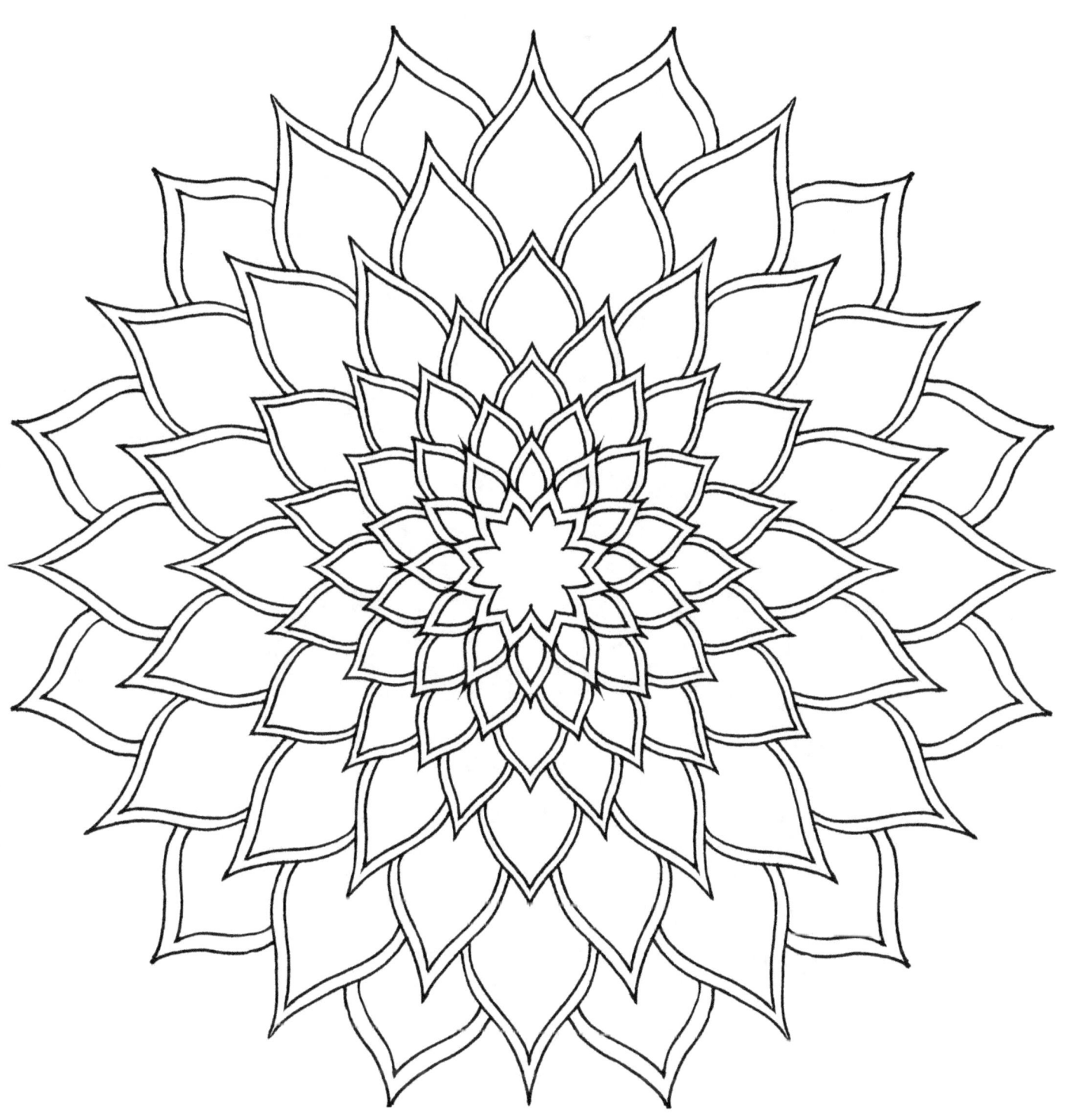

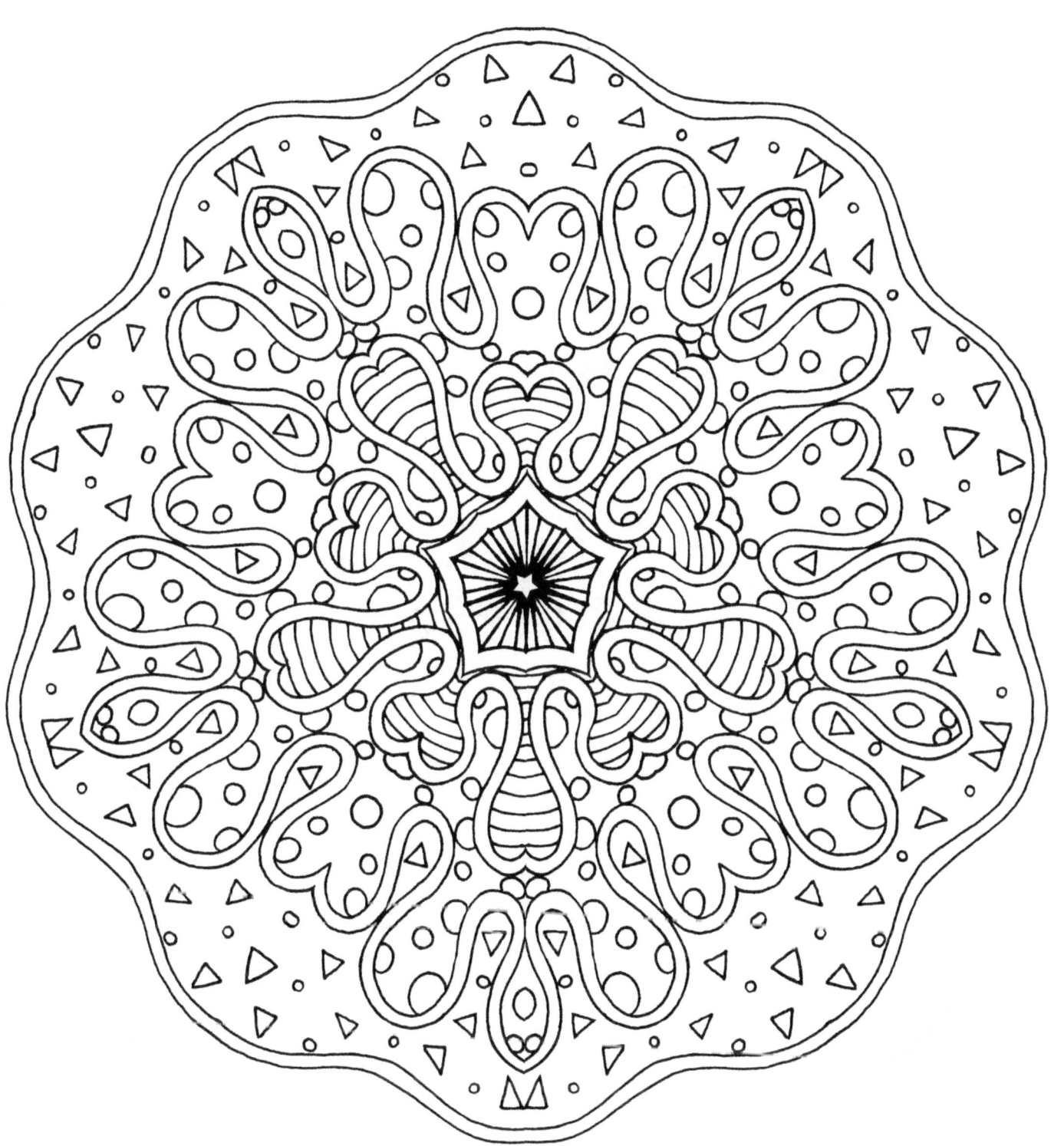

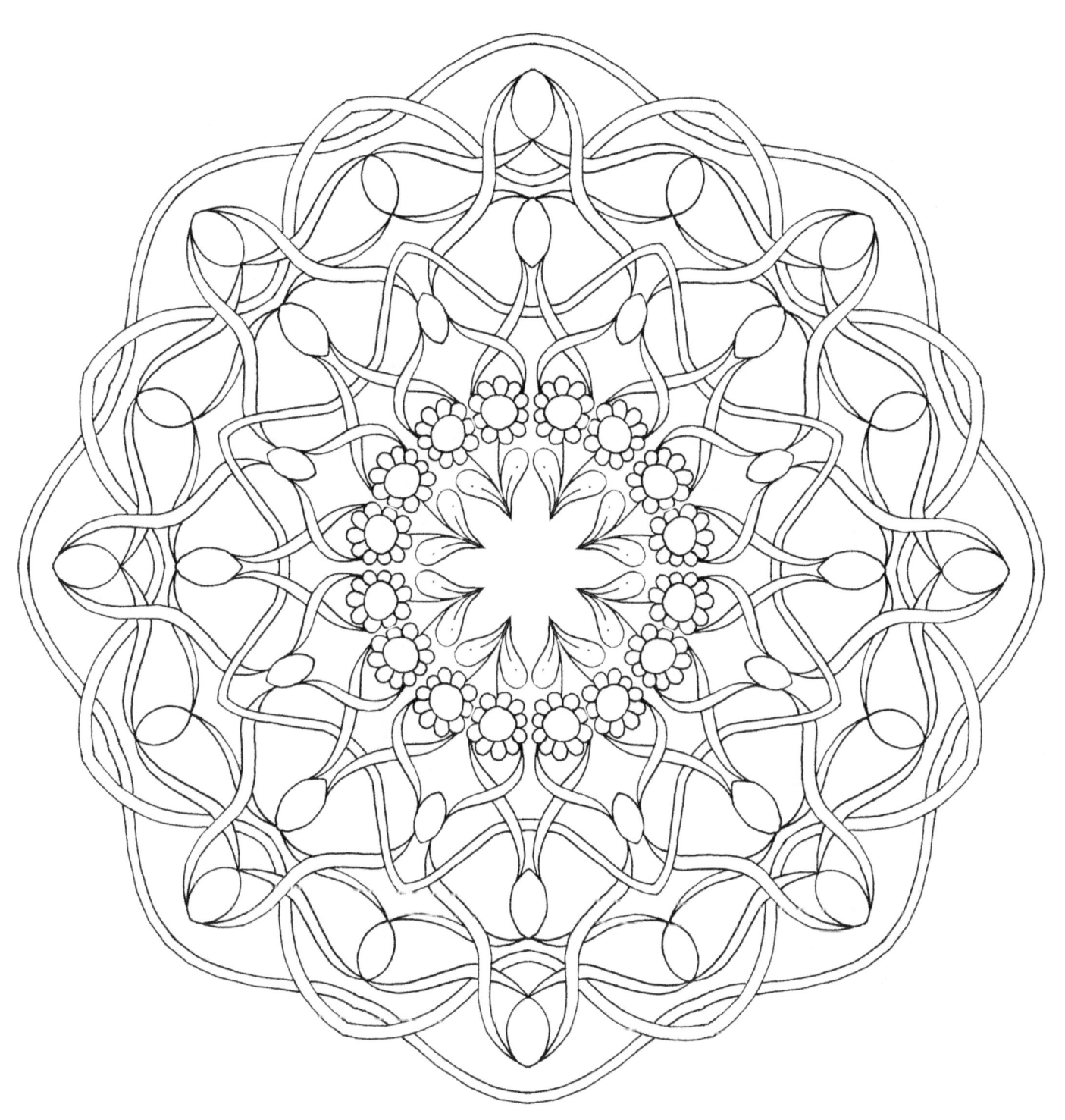

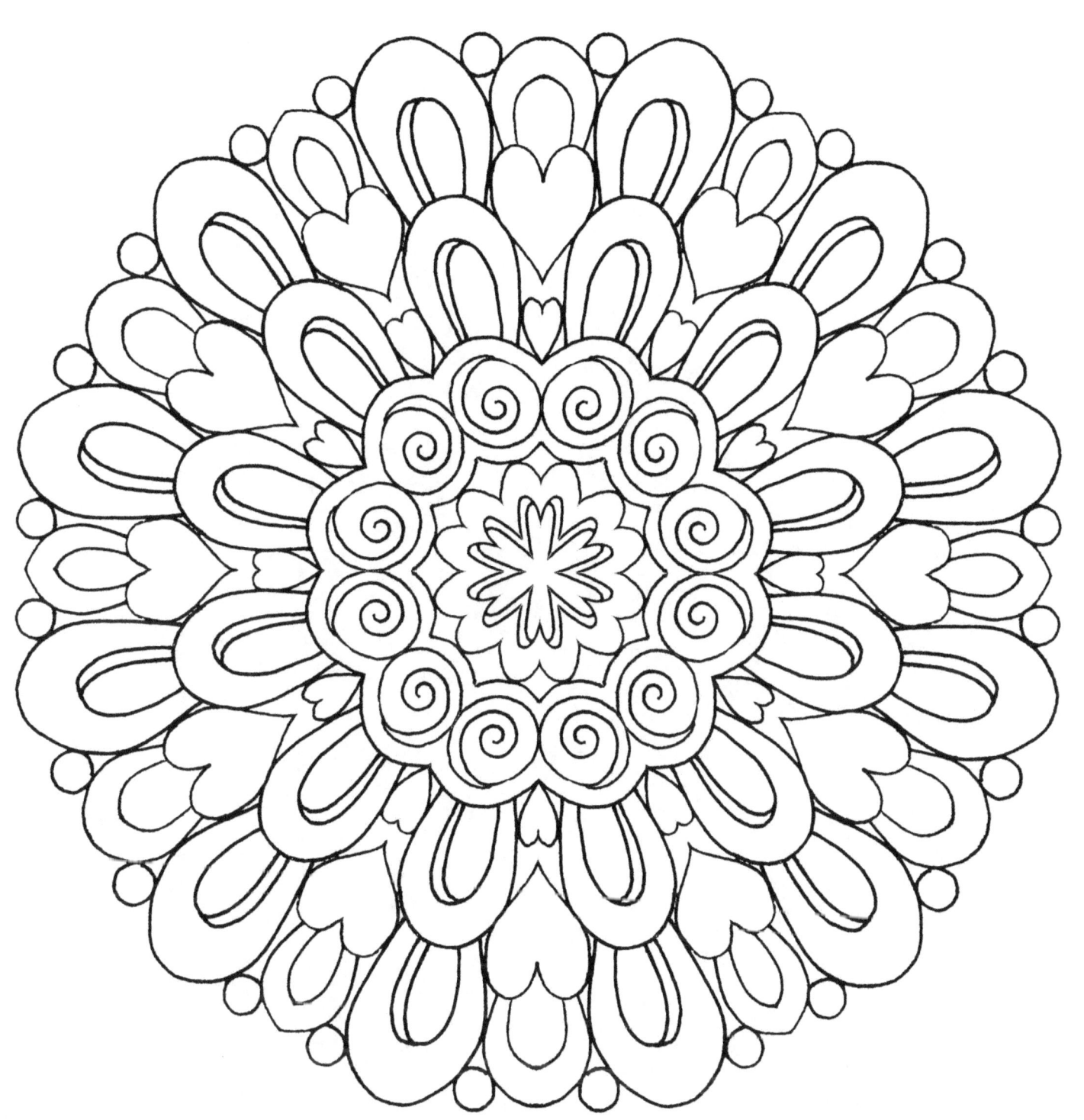

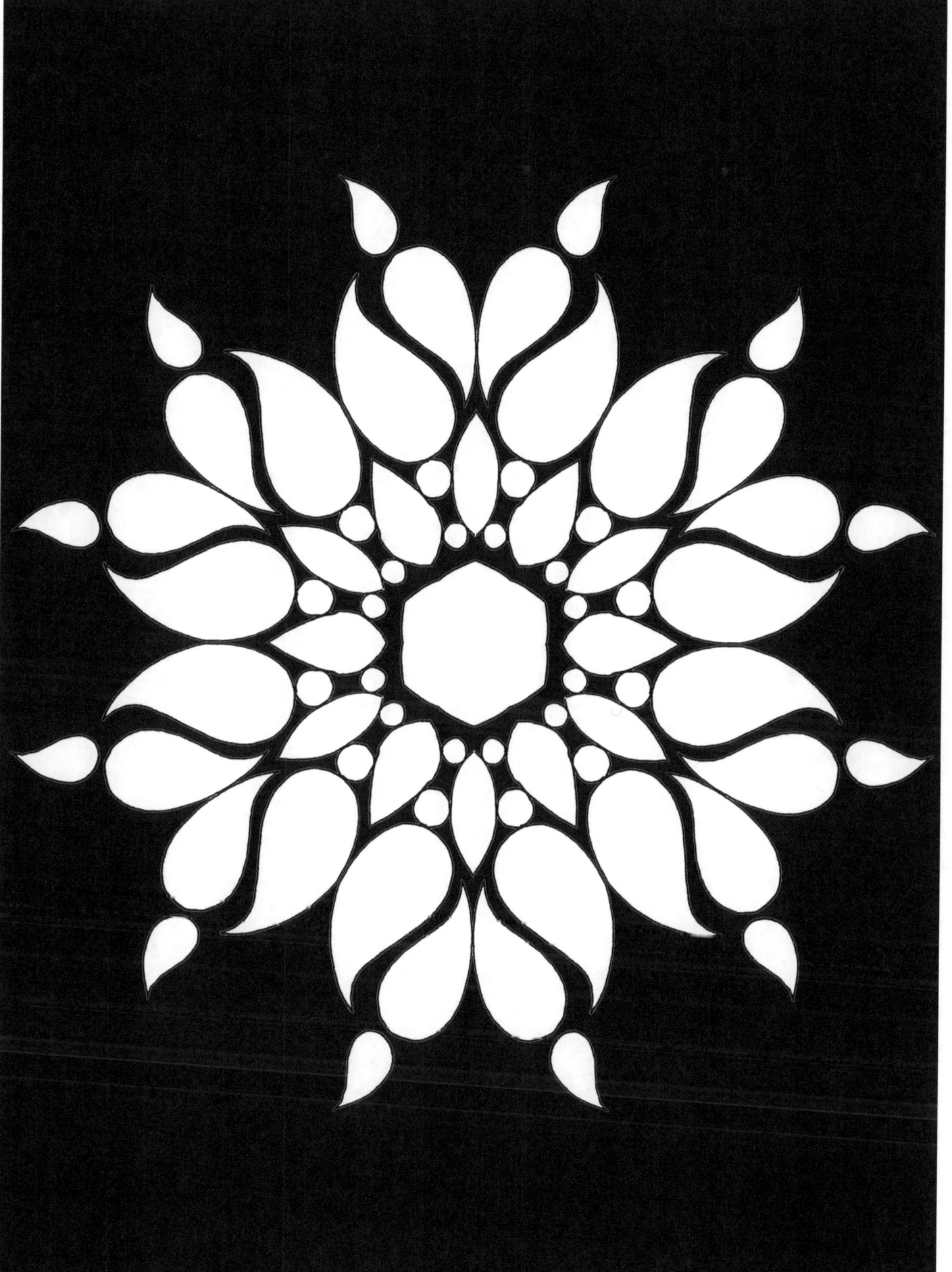

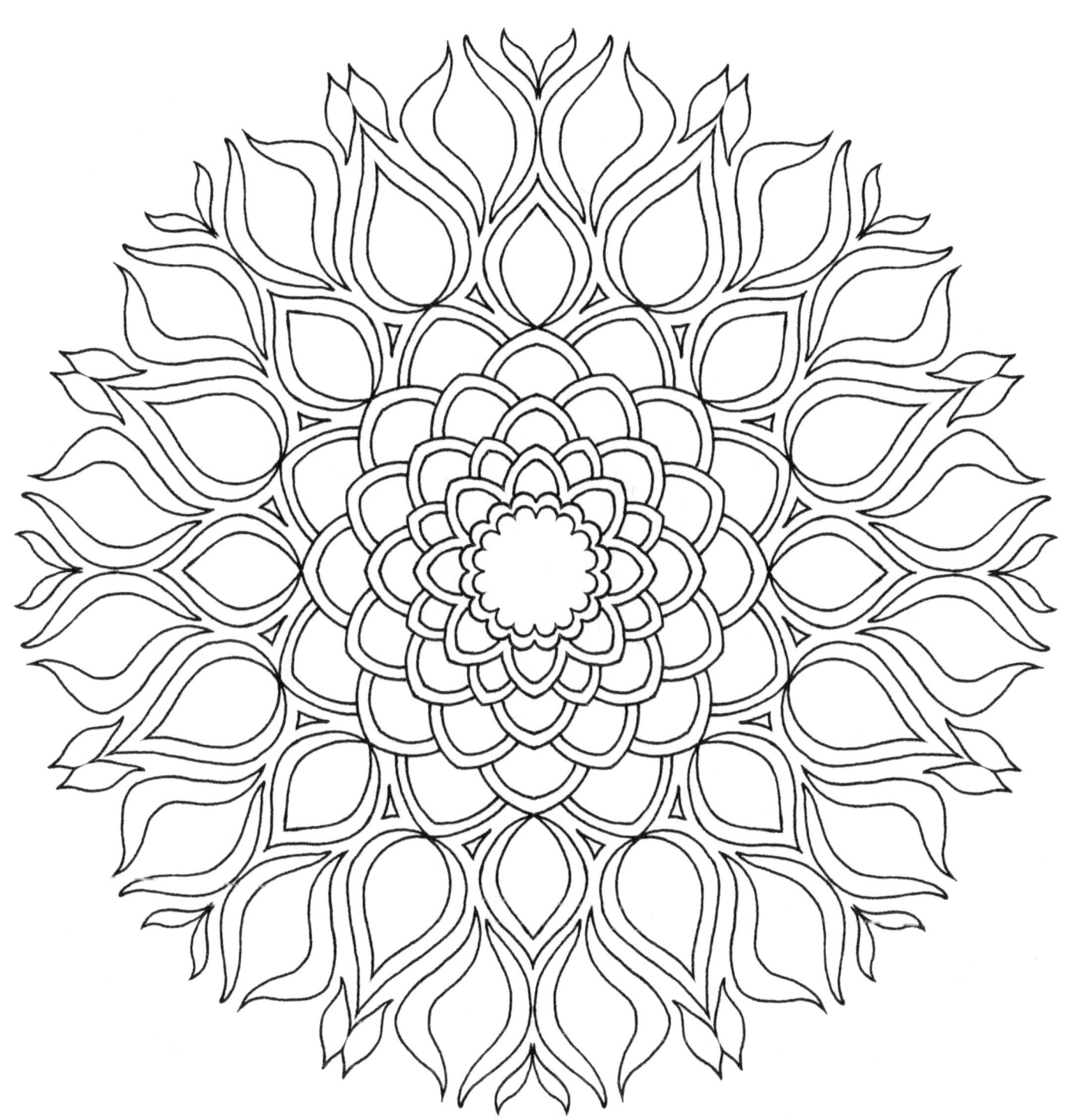

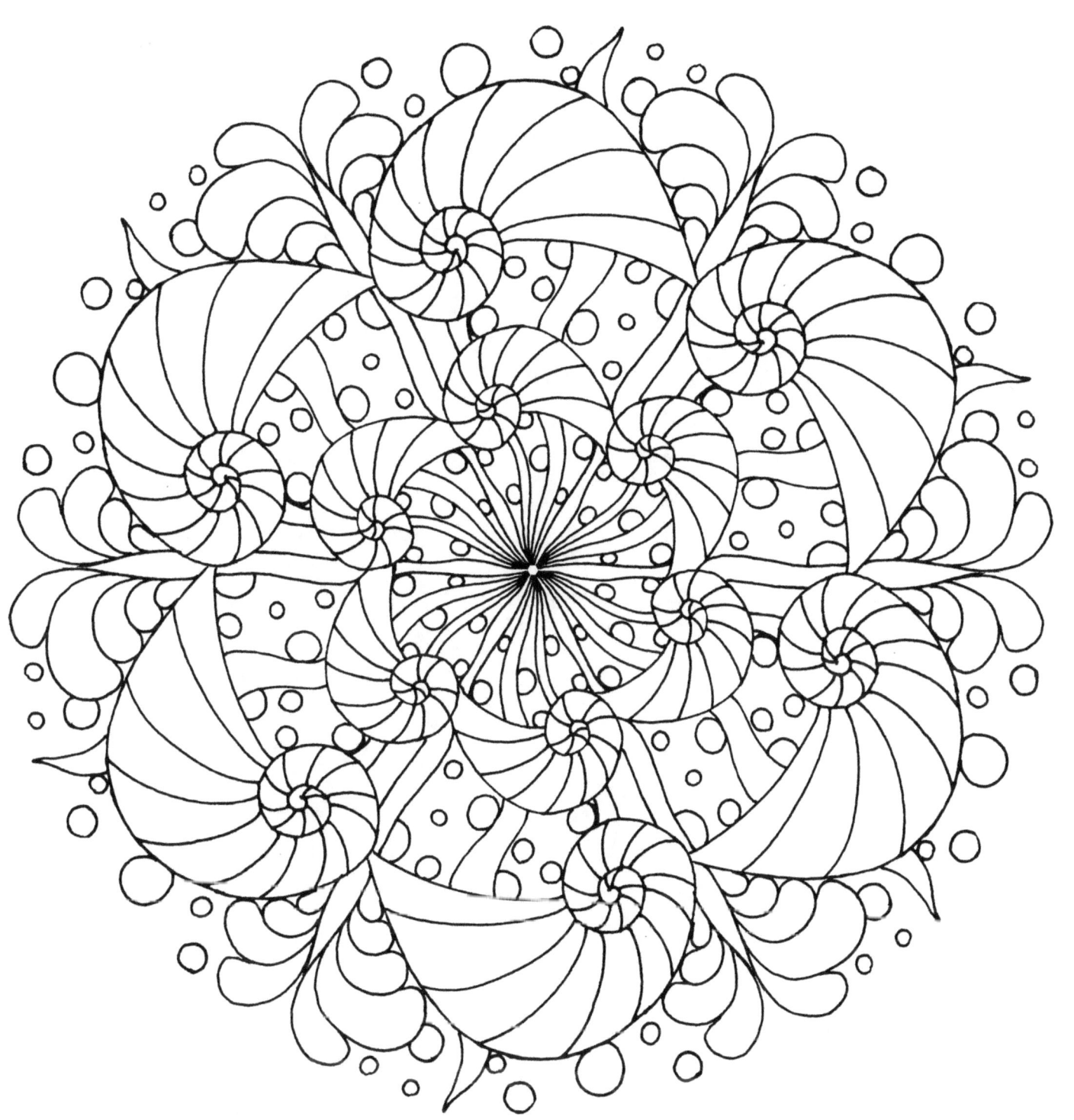

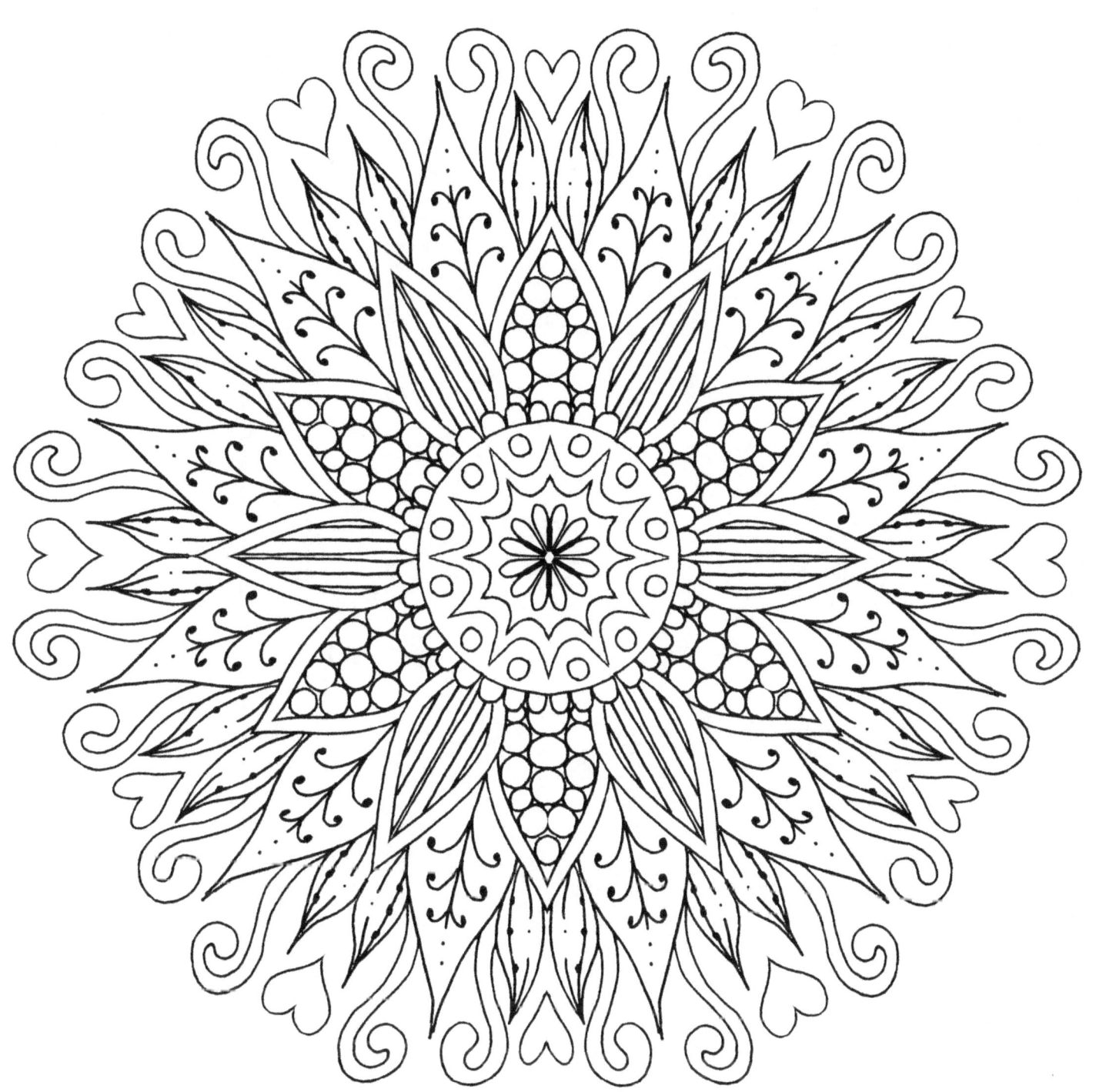

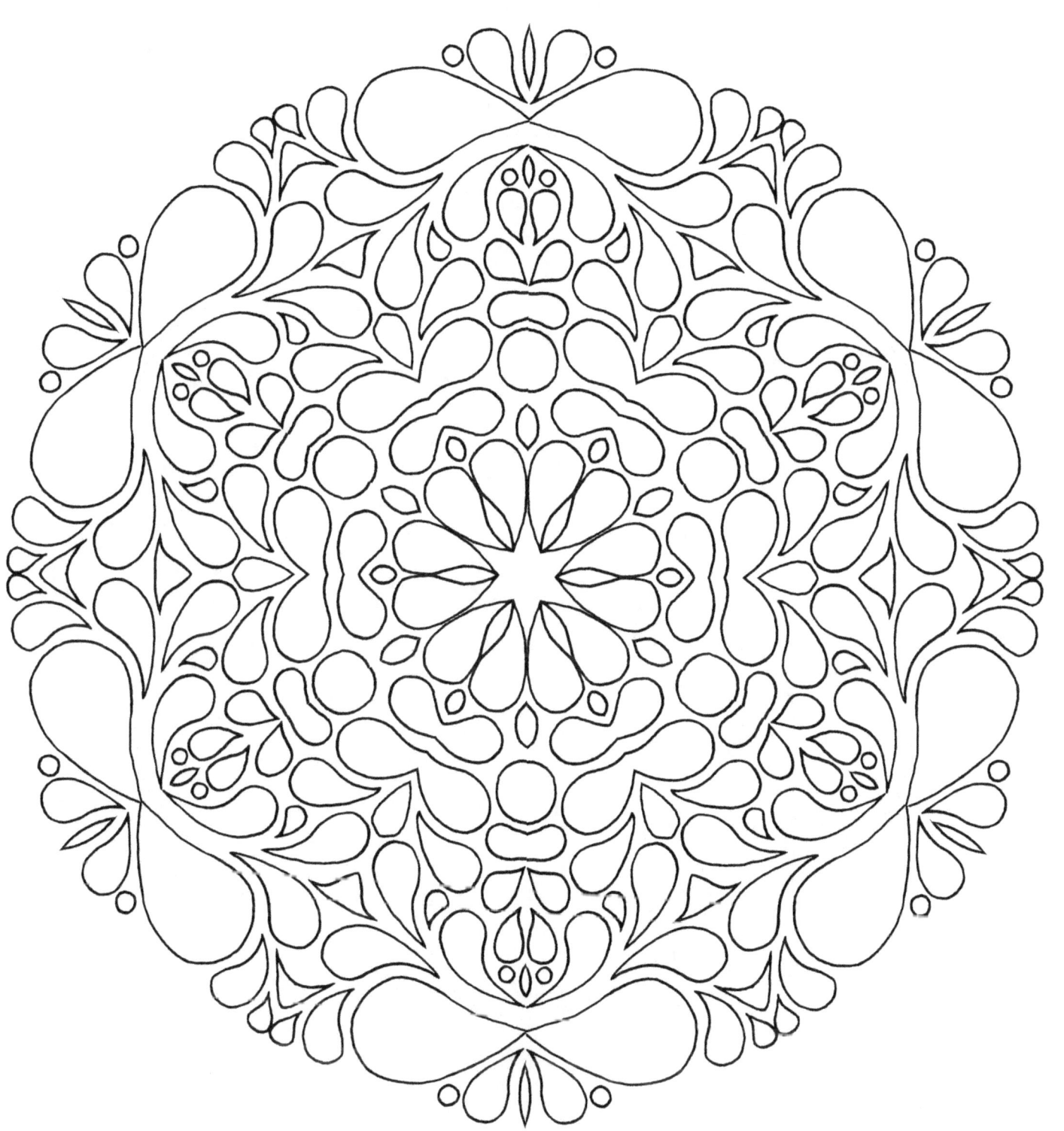

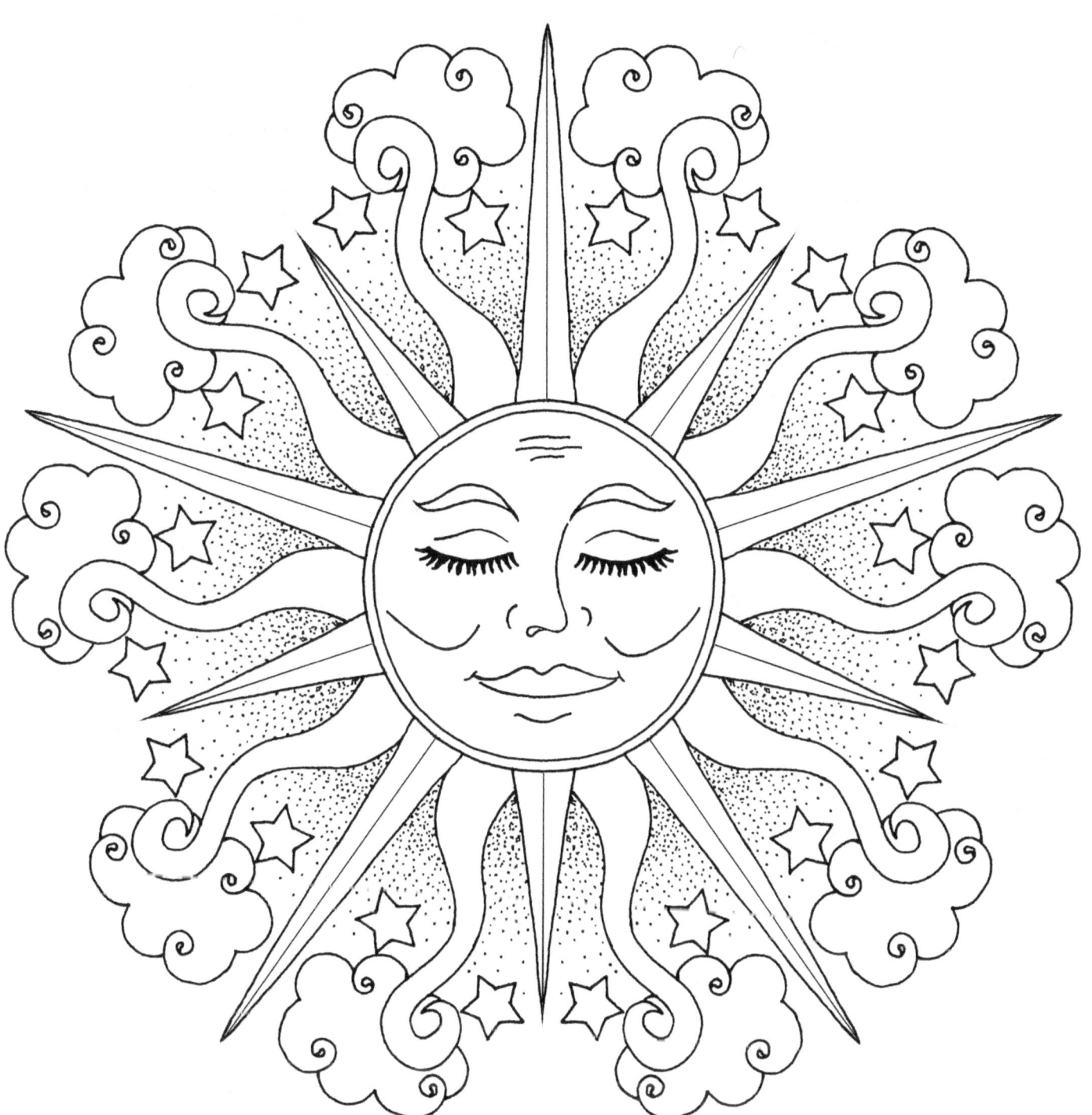

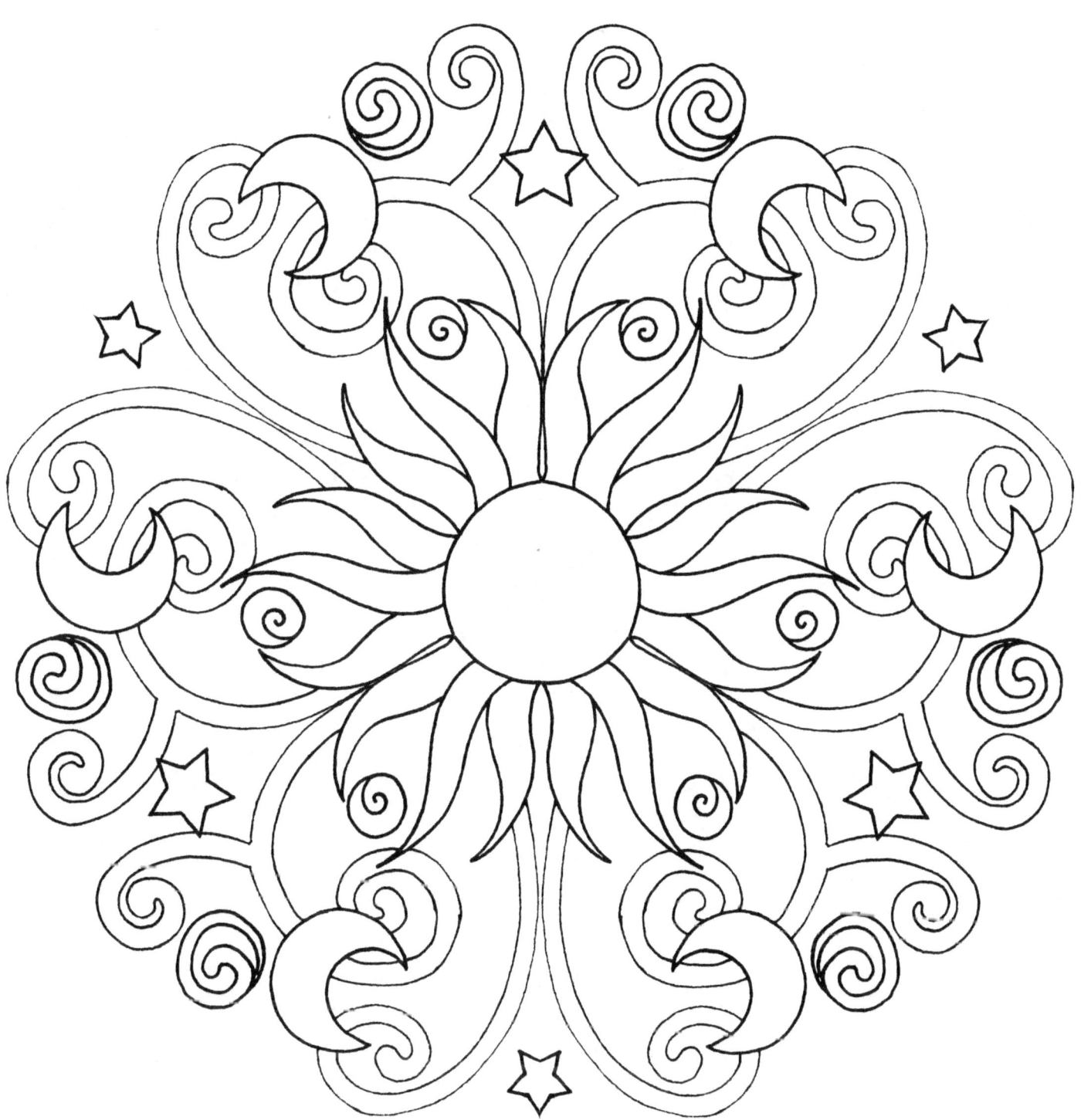

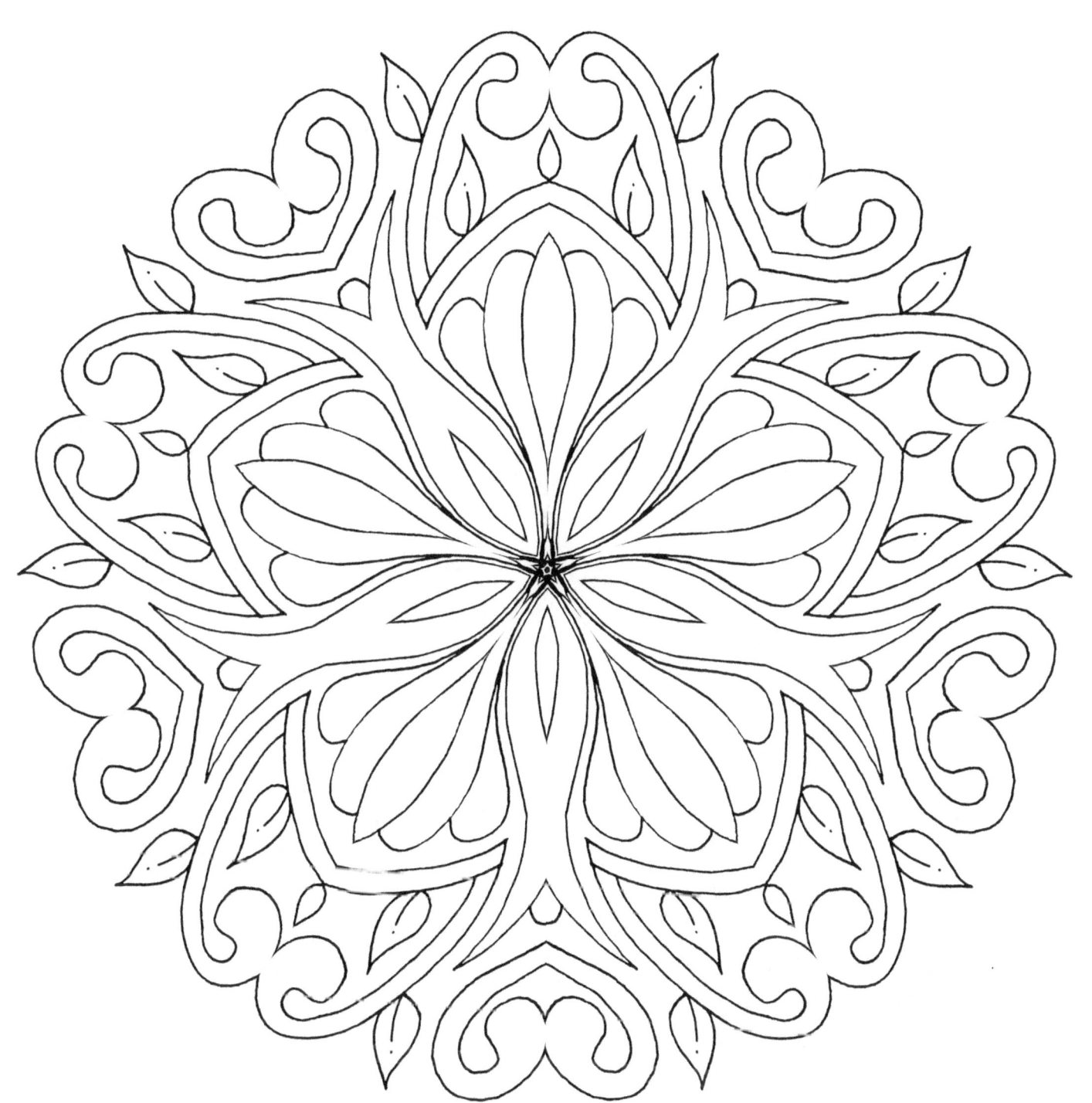

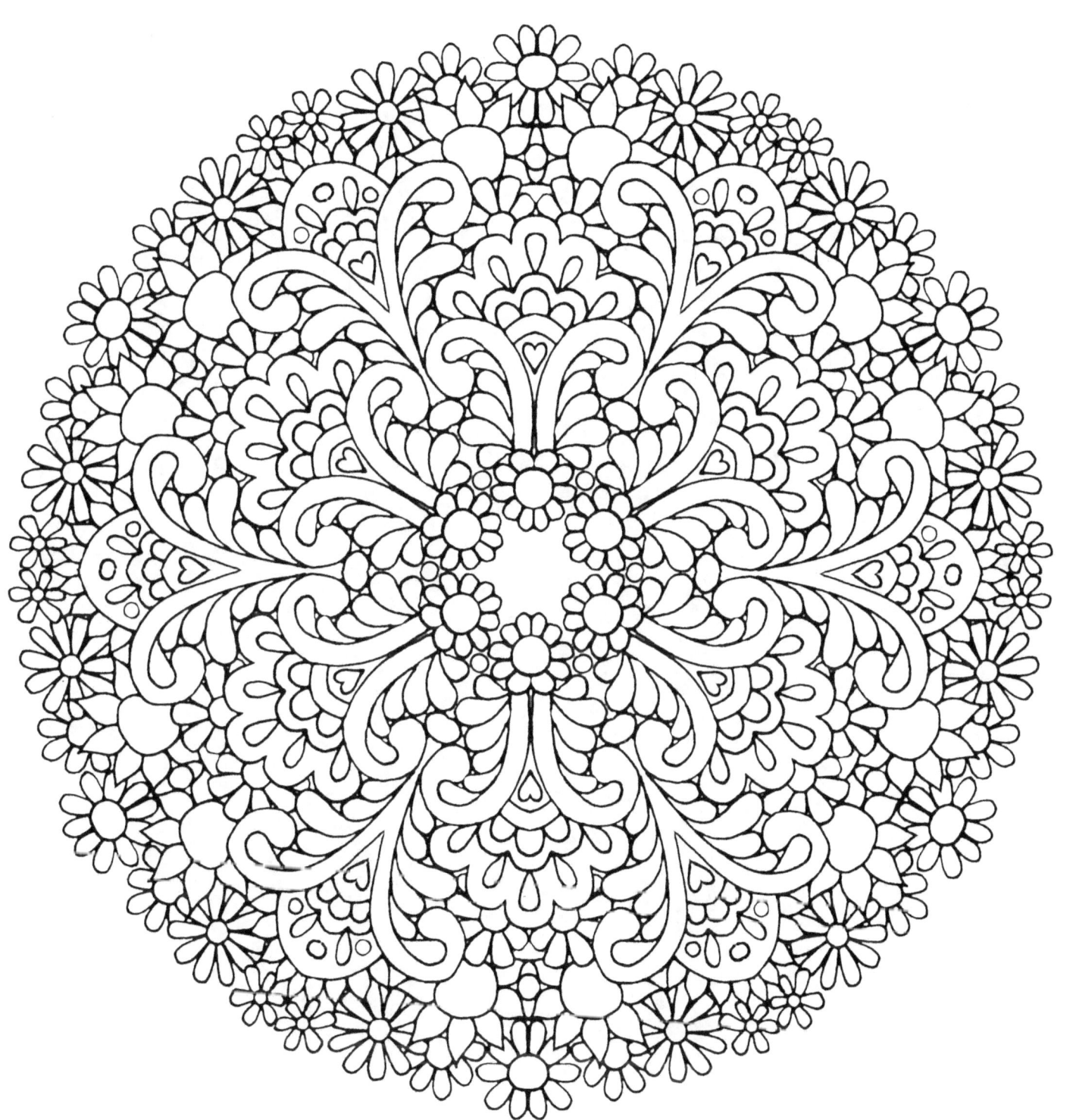

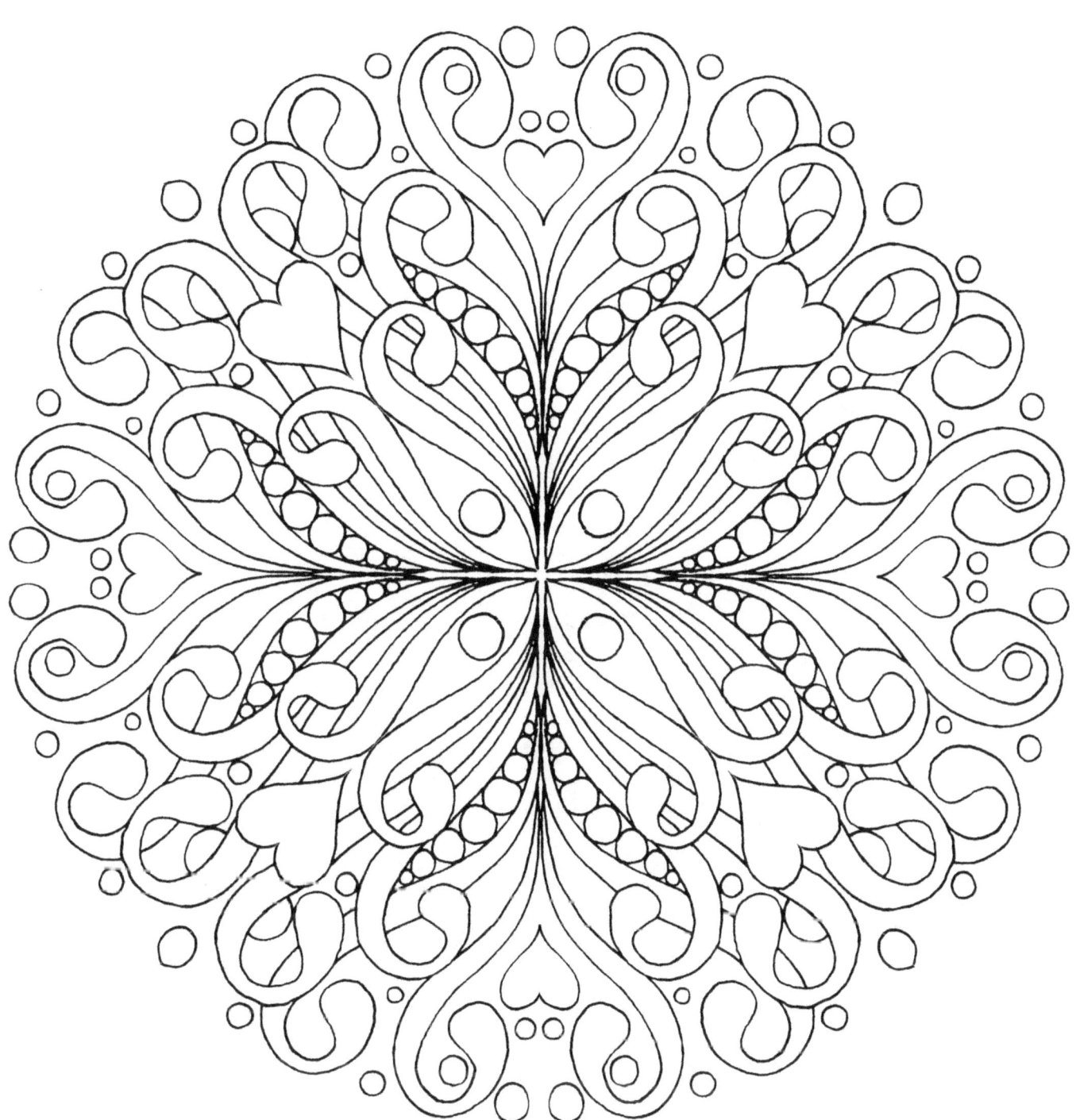

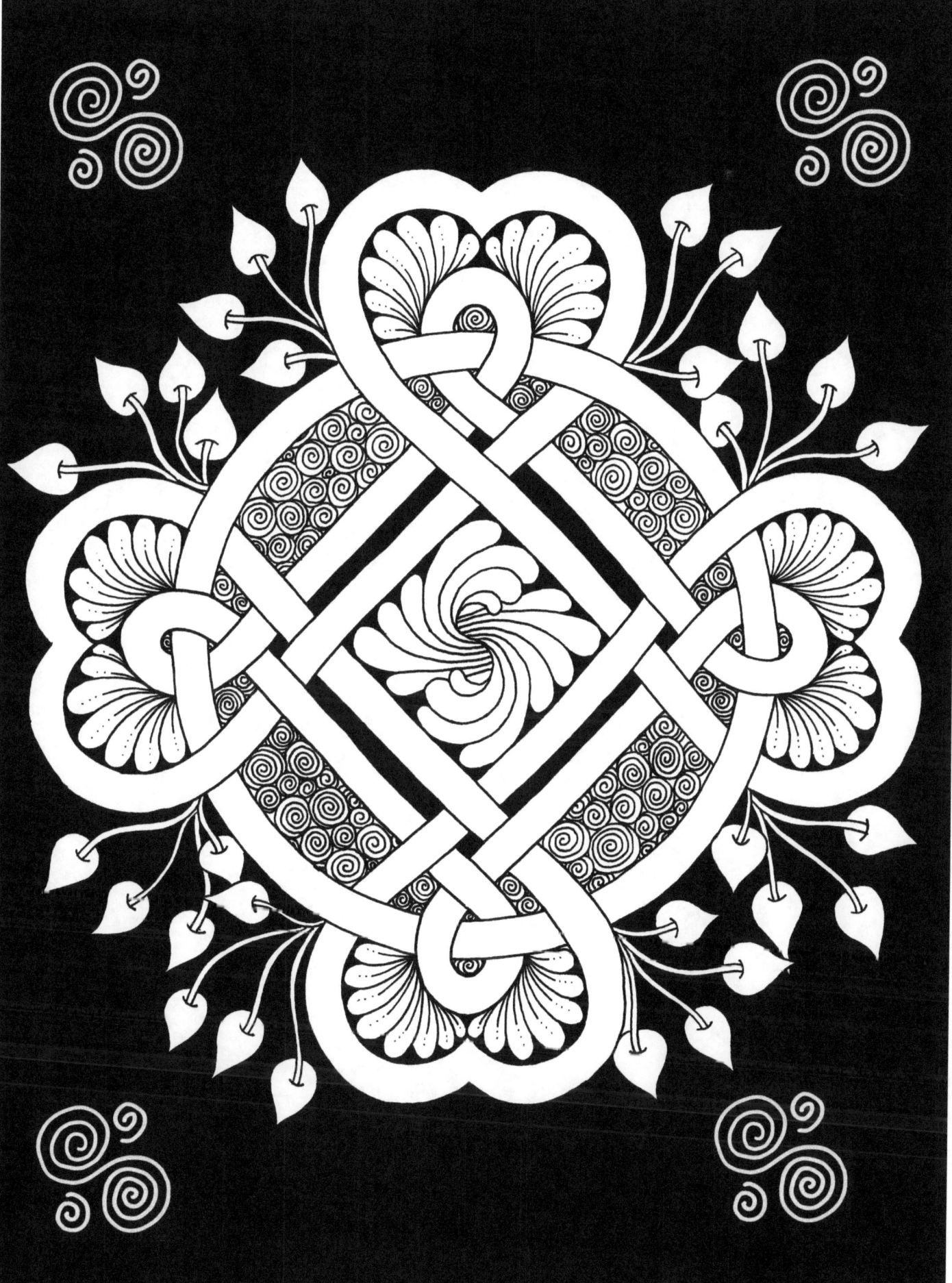

©Tabitha Barnett 2016

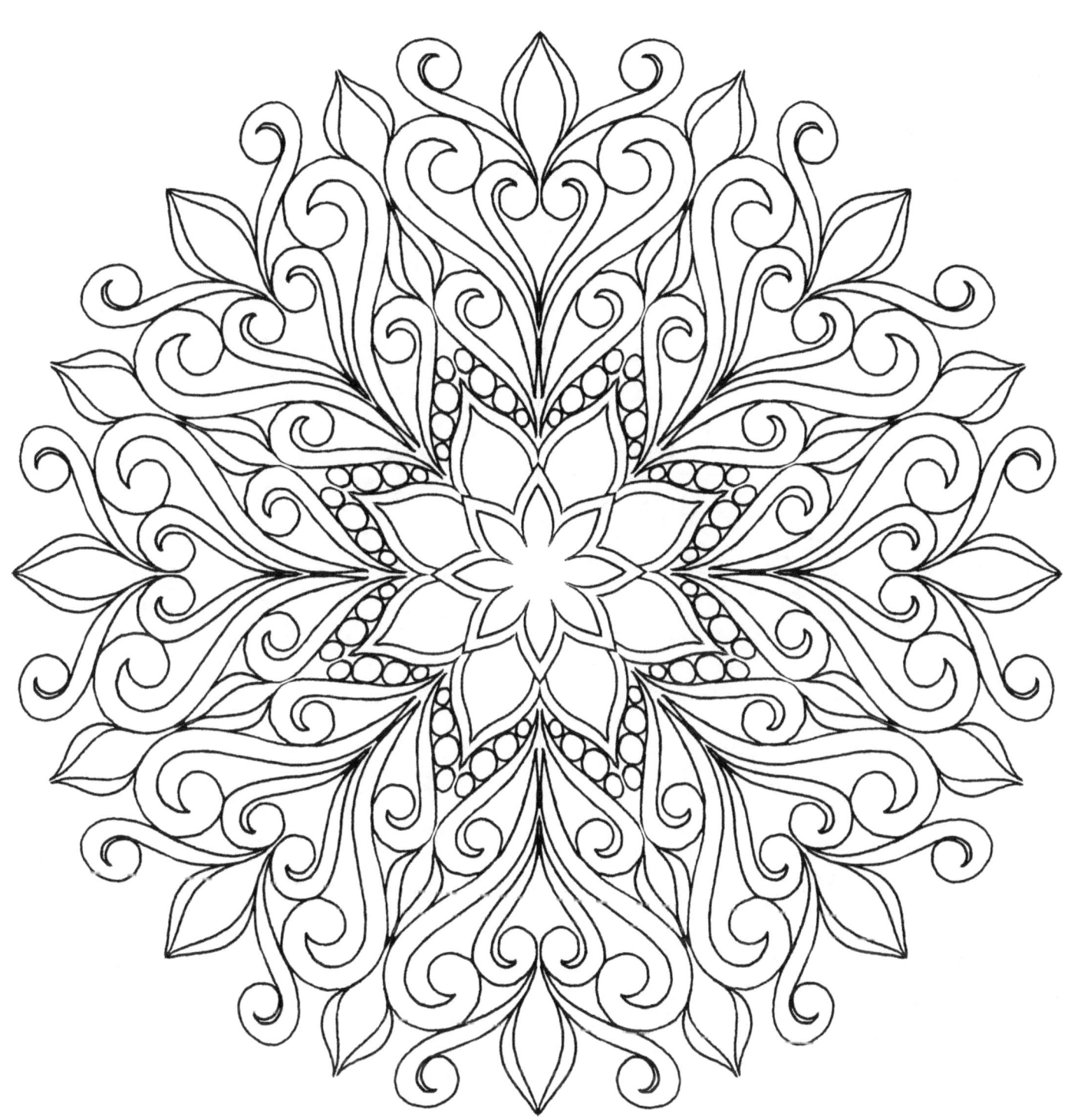

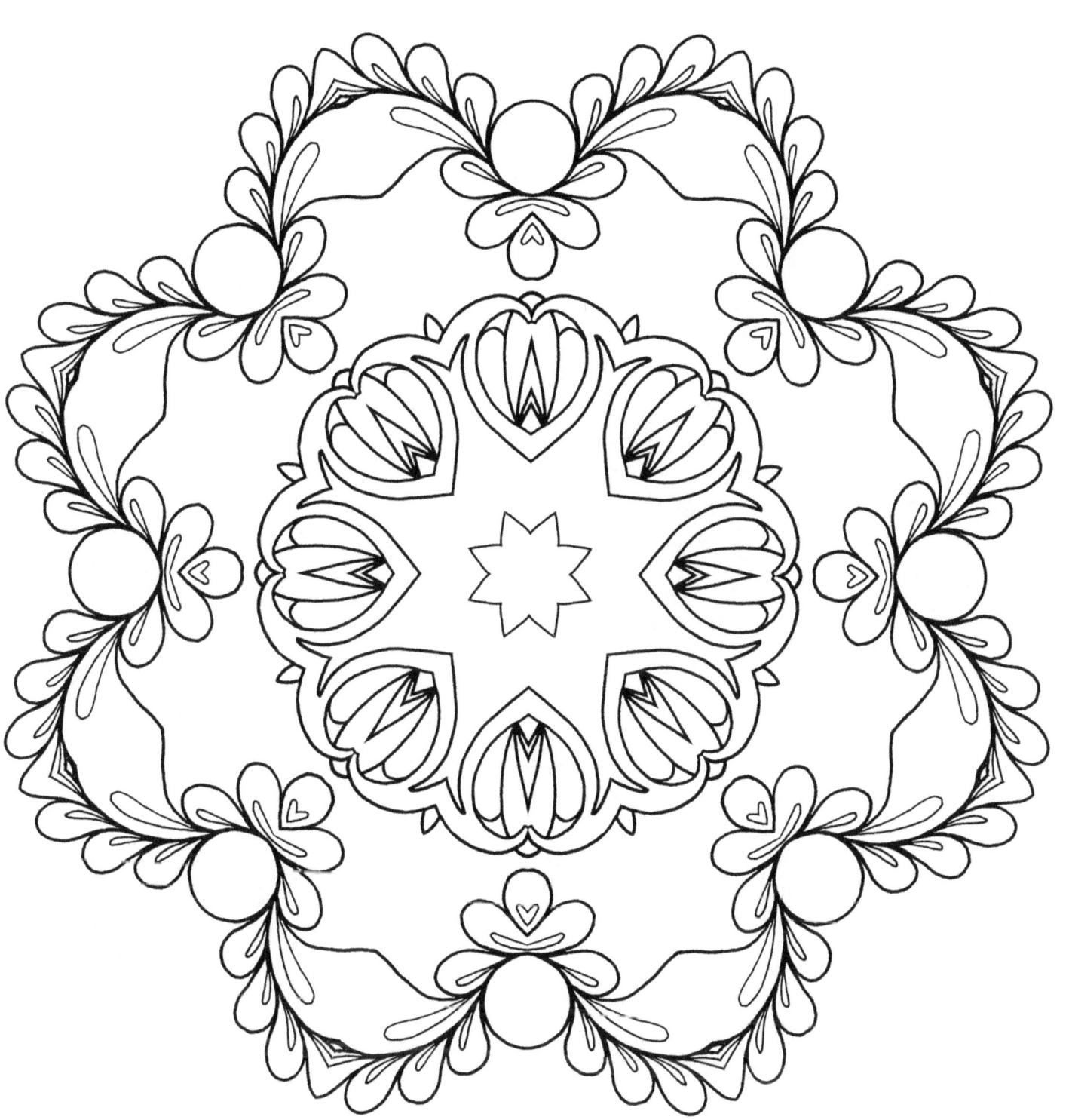

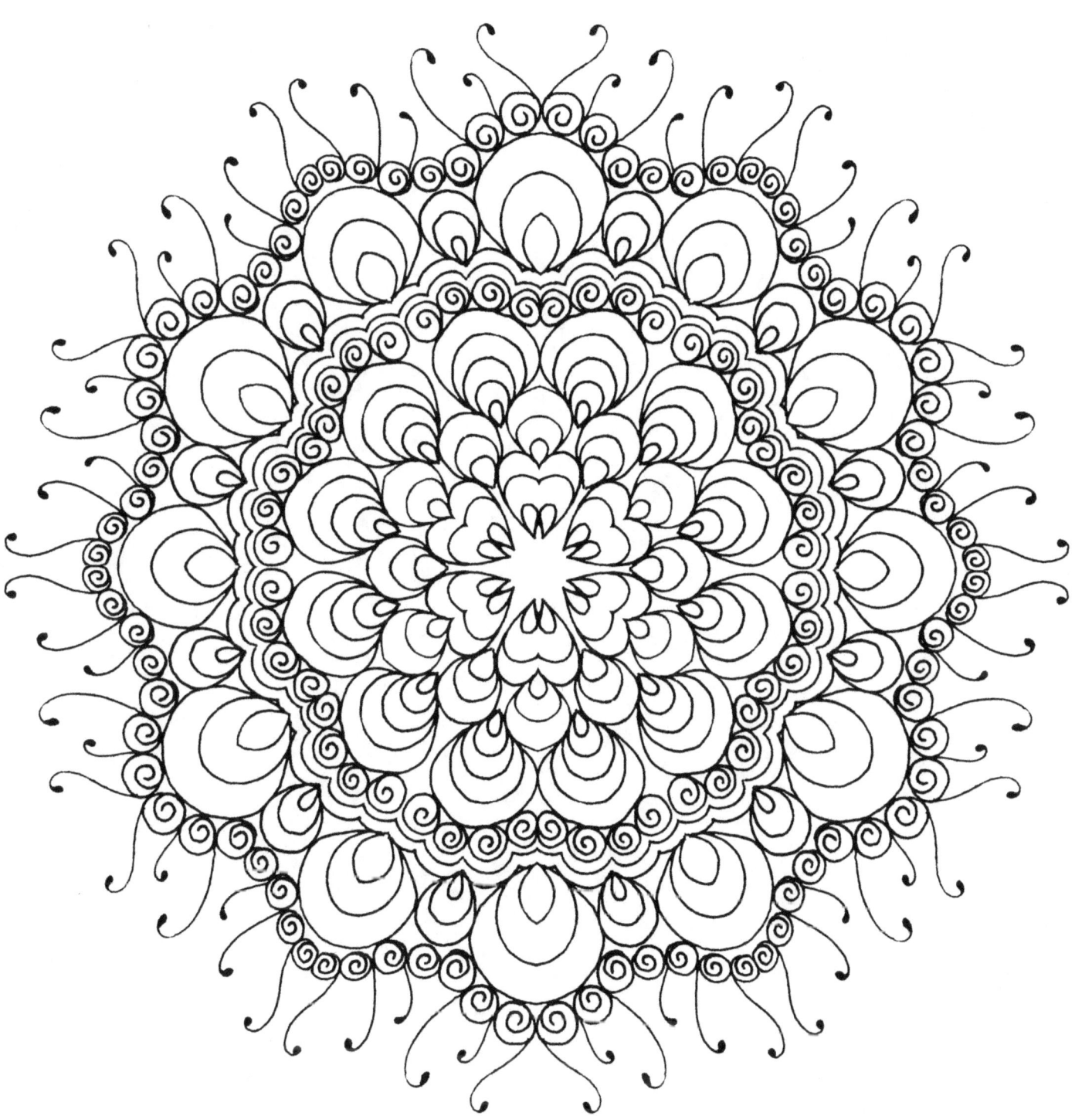

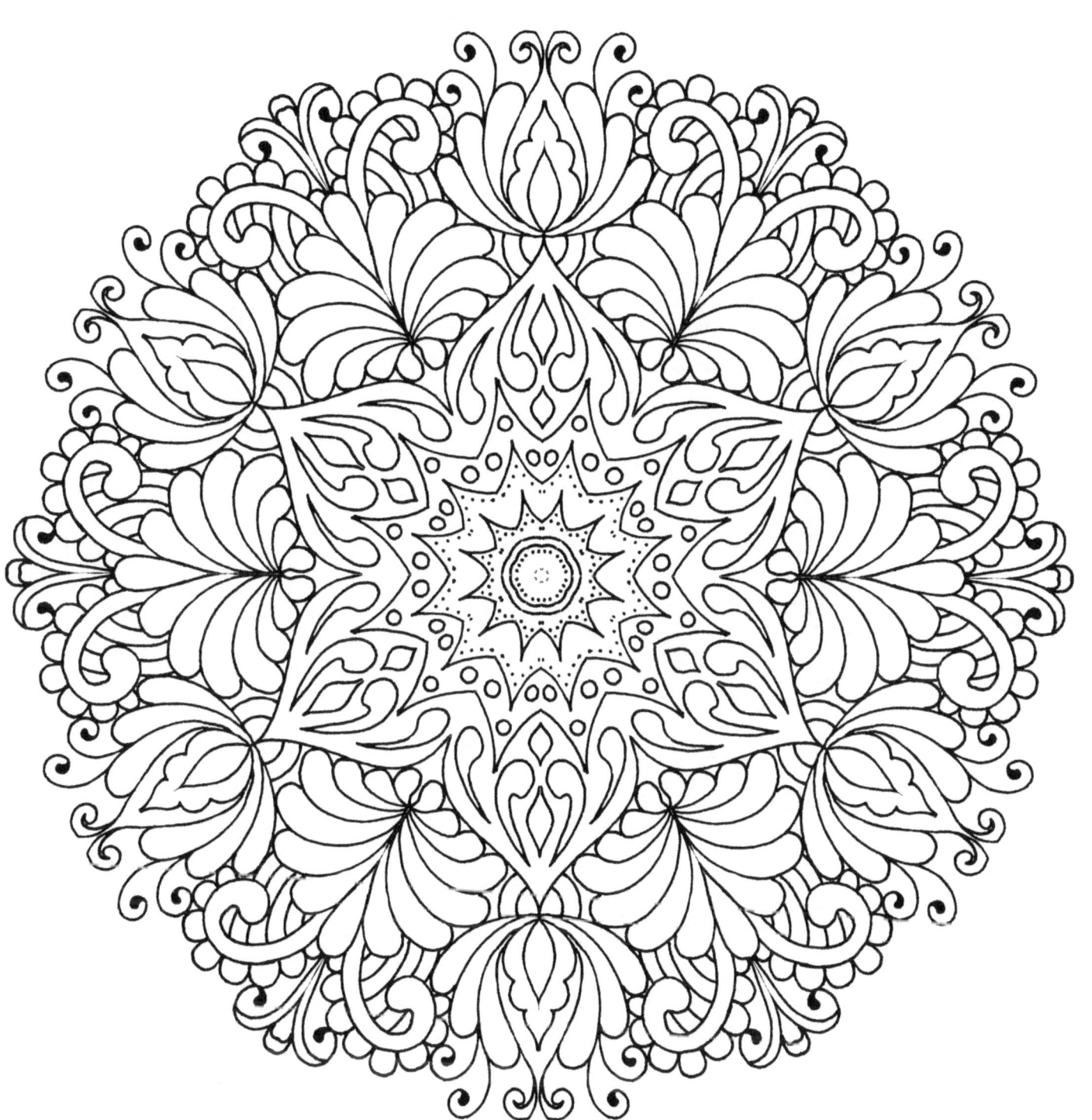

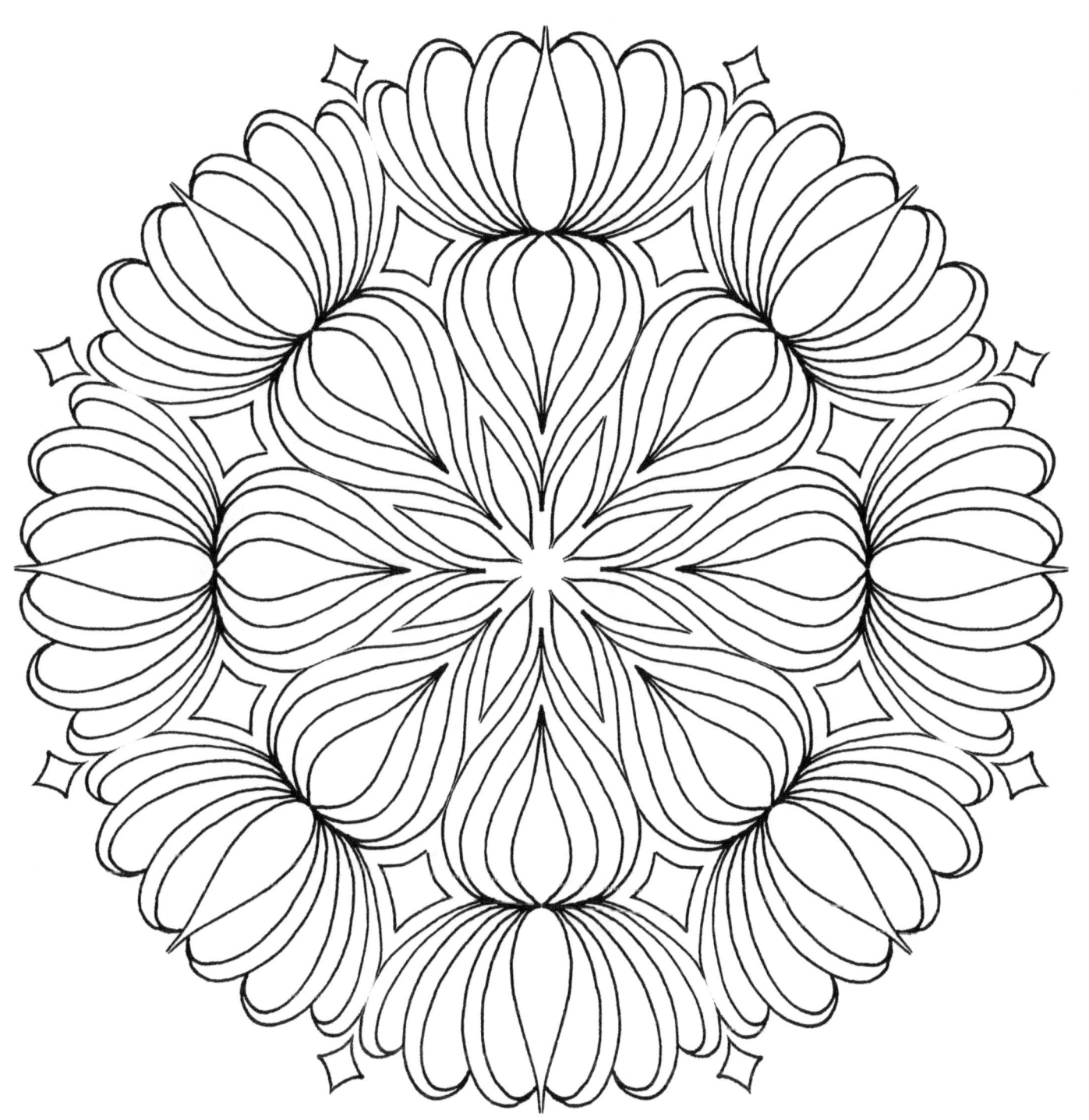

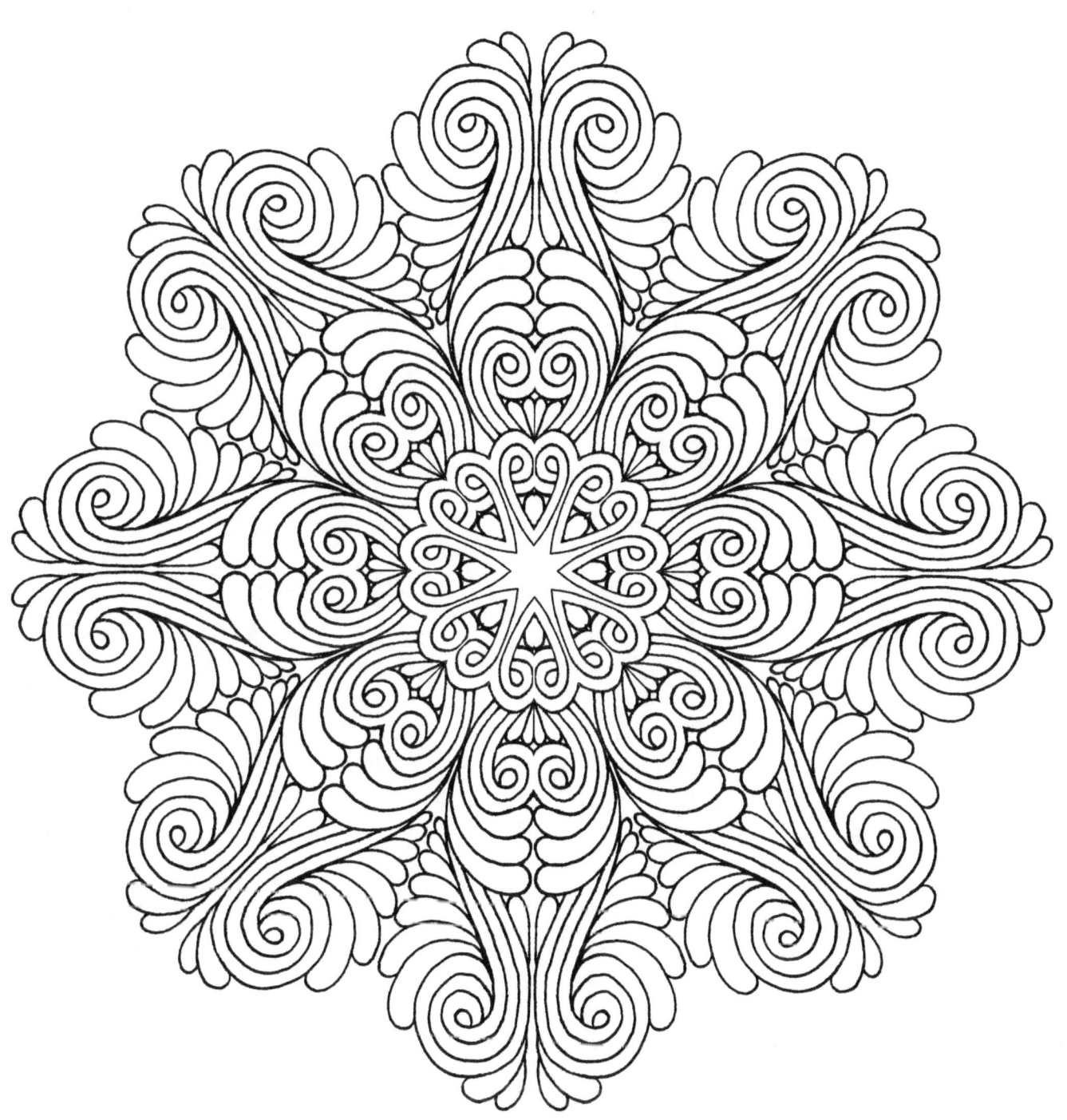

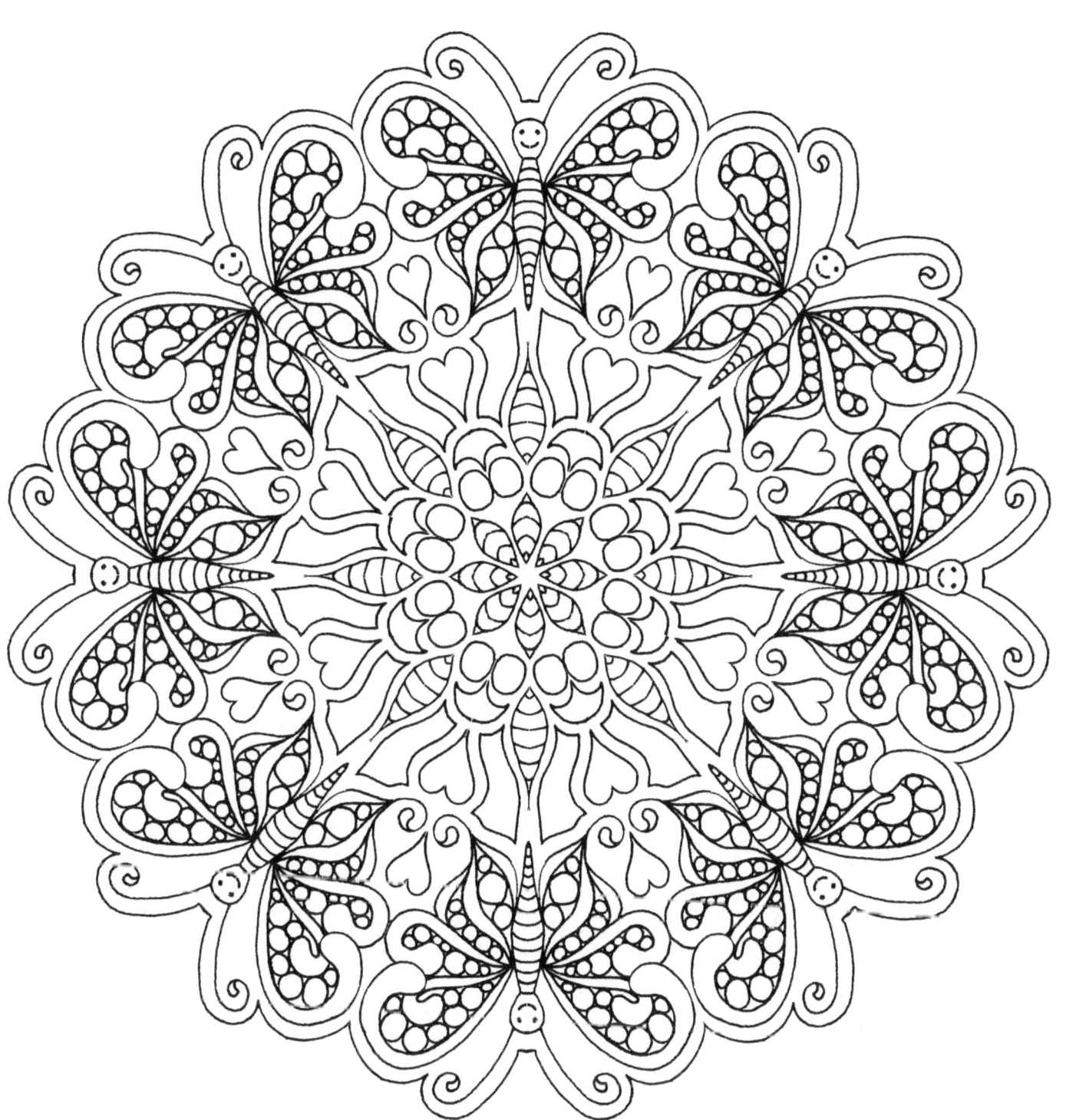

©Tabitha Barnett 2016

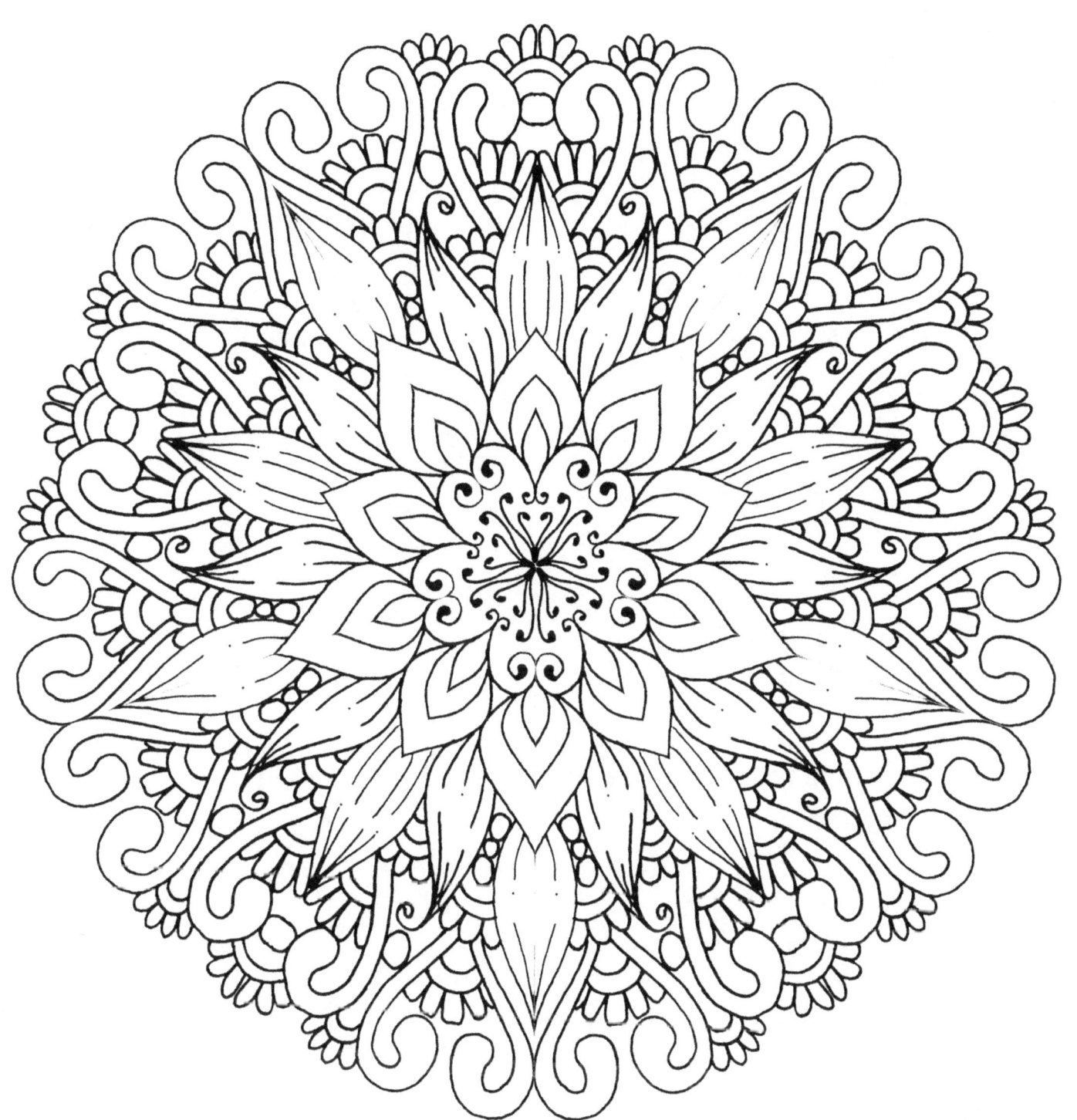

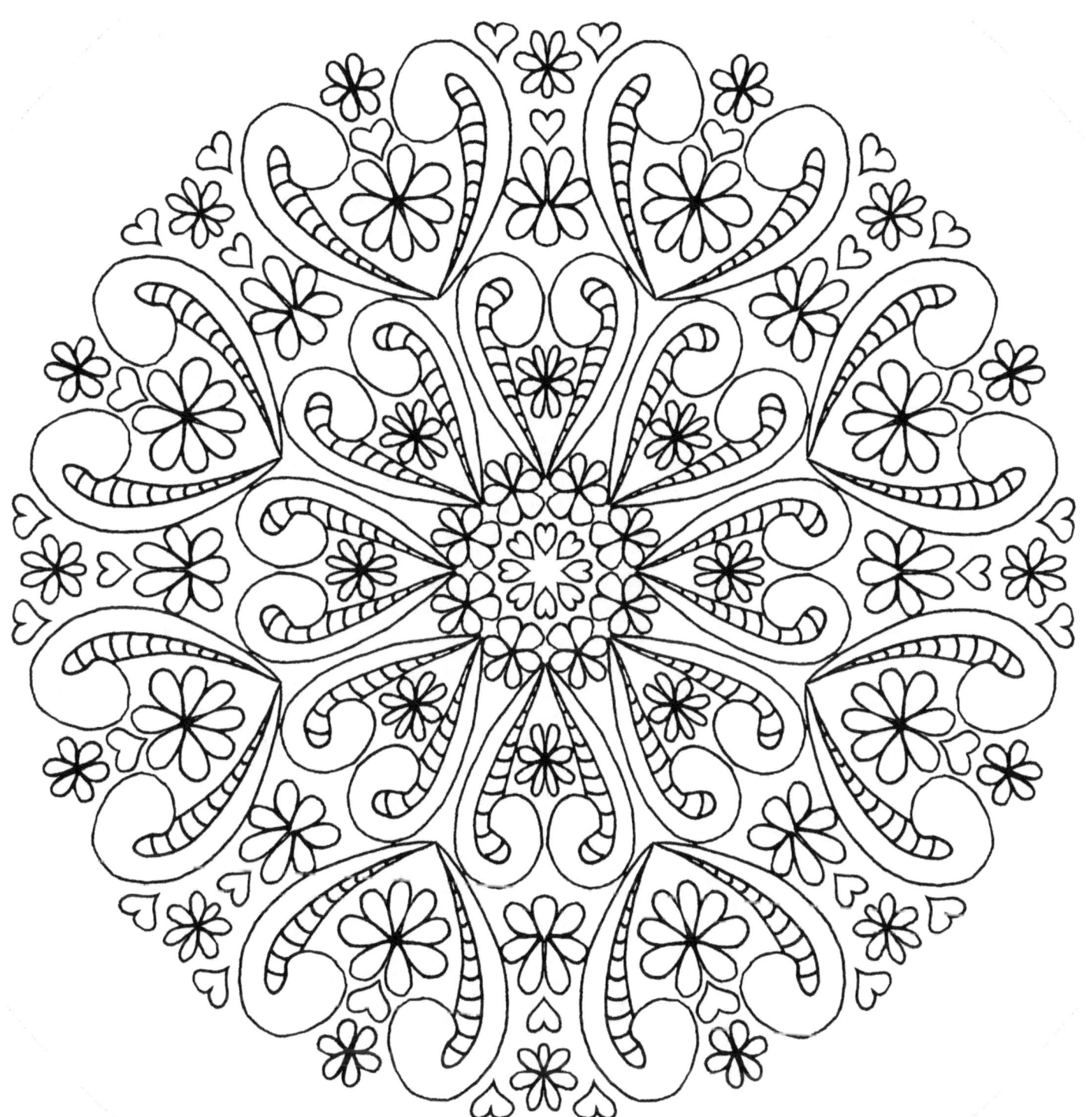

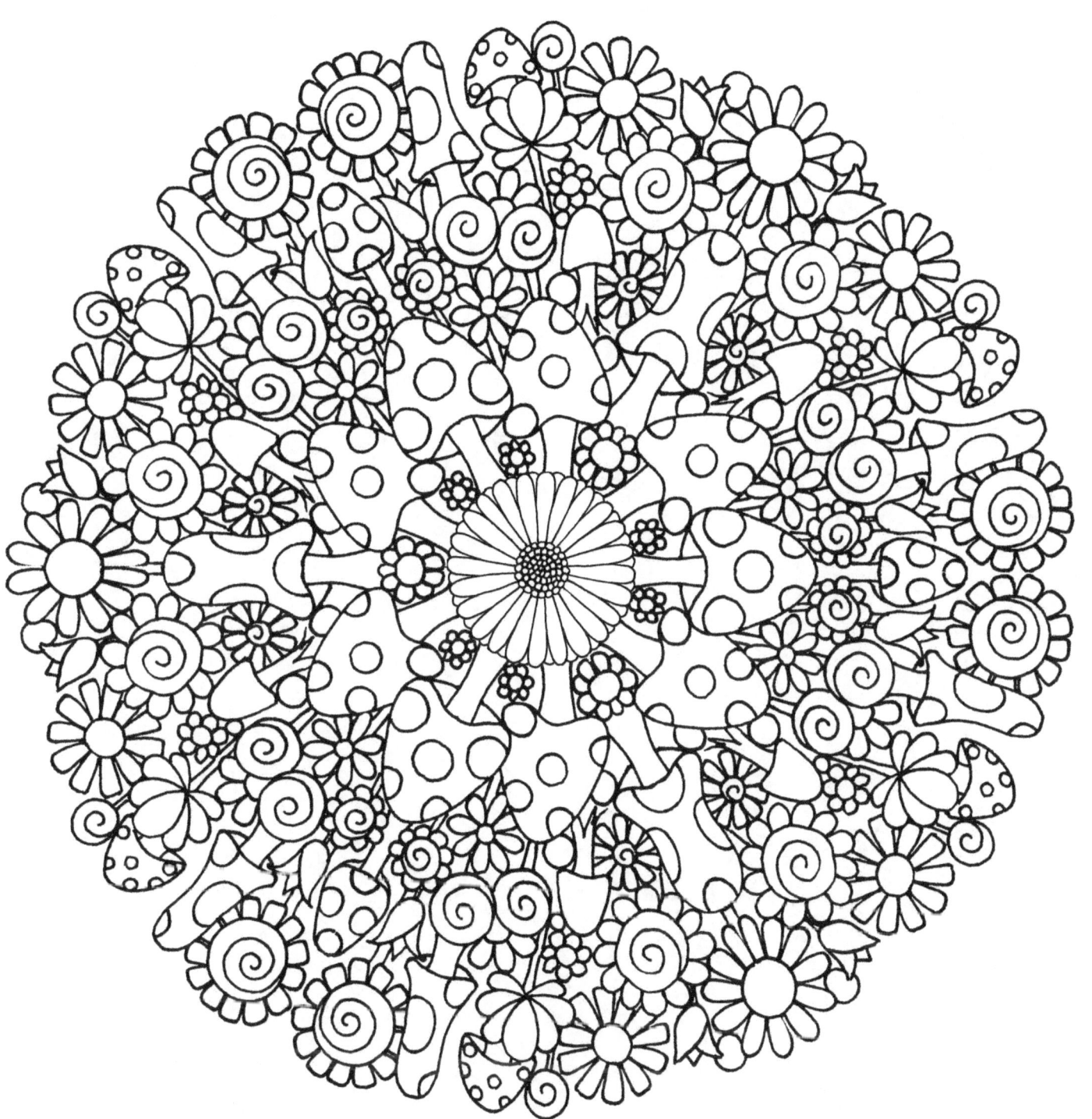

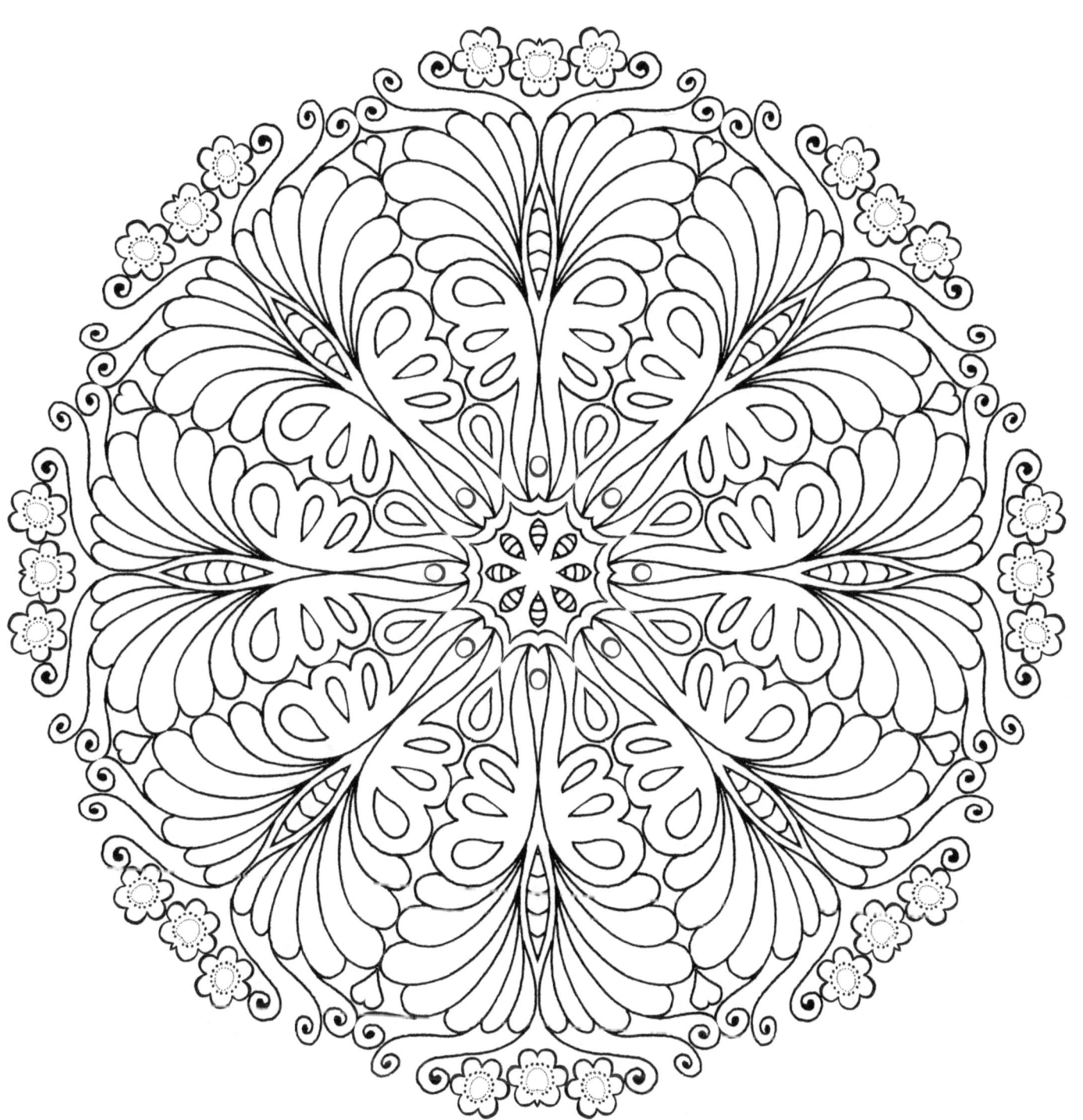

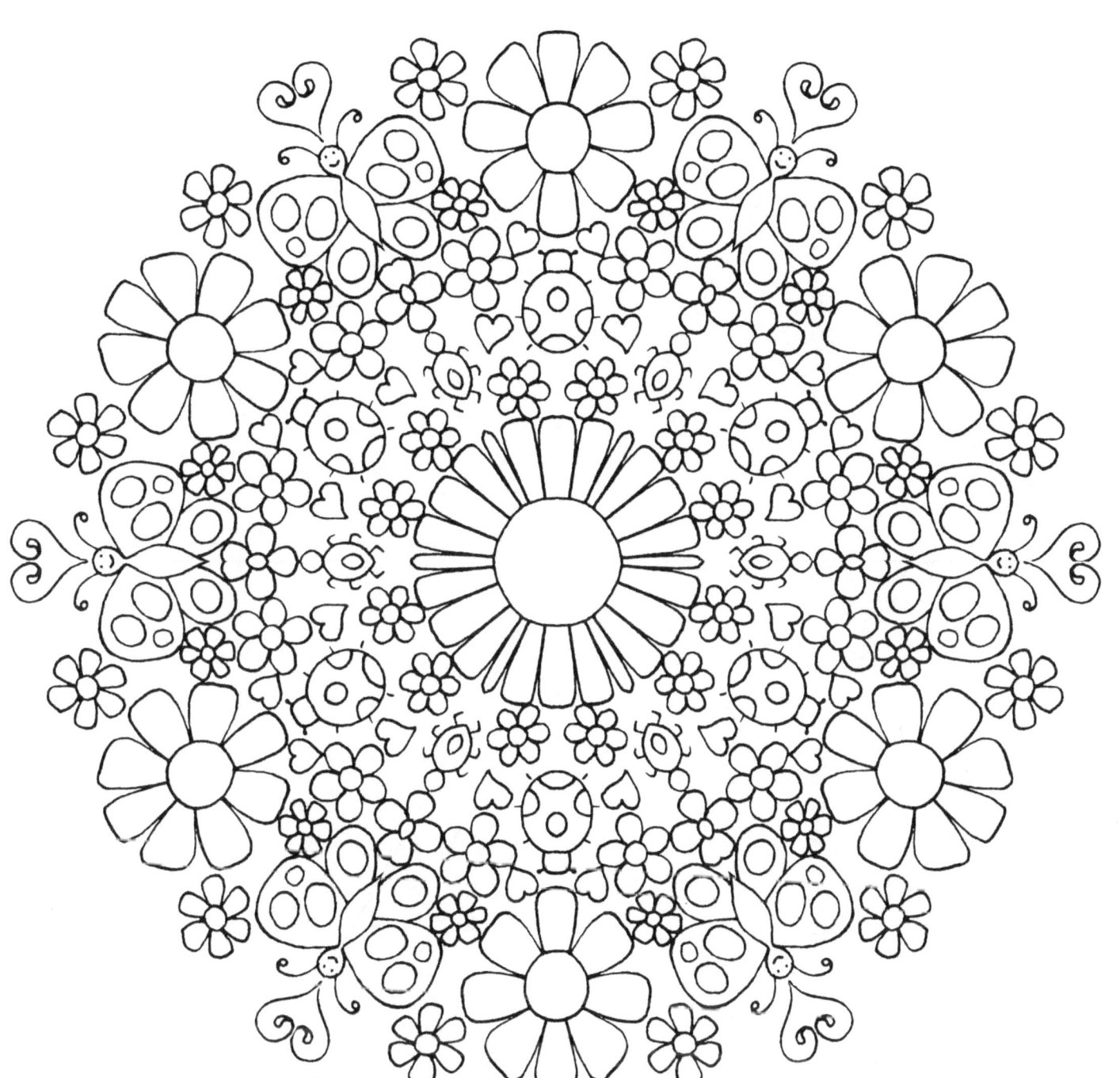

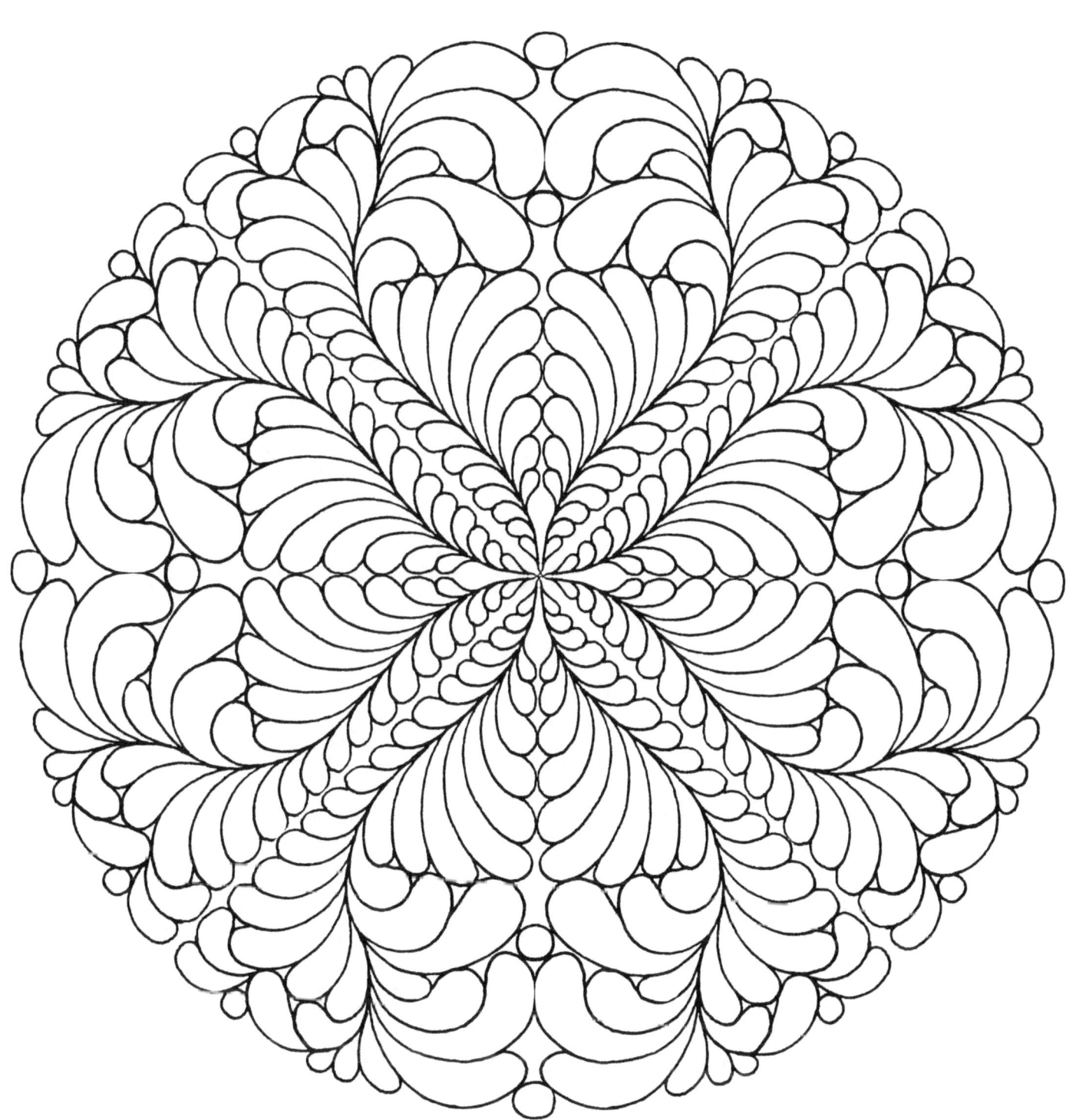

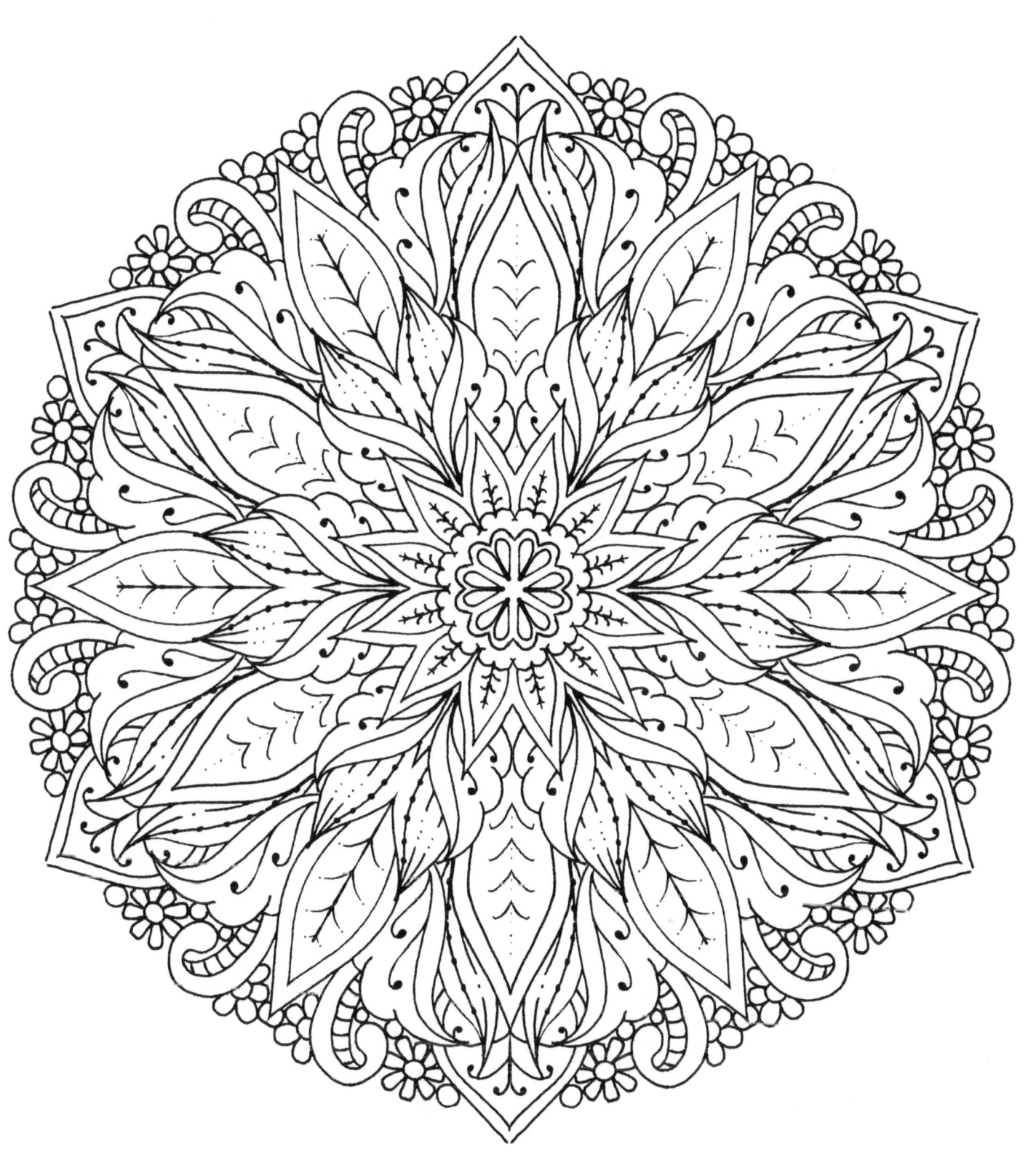

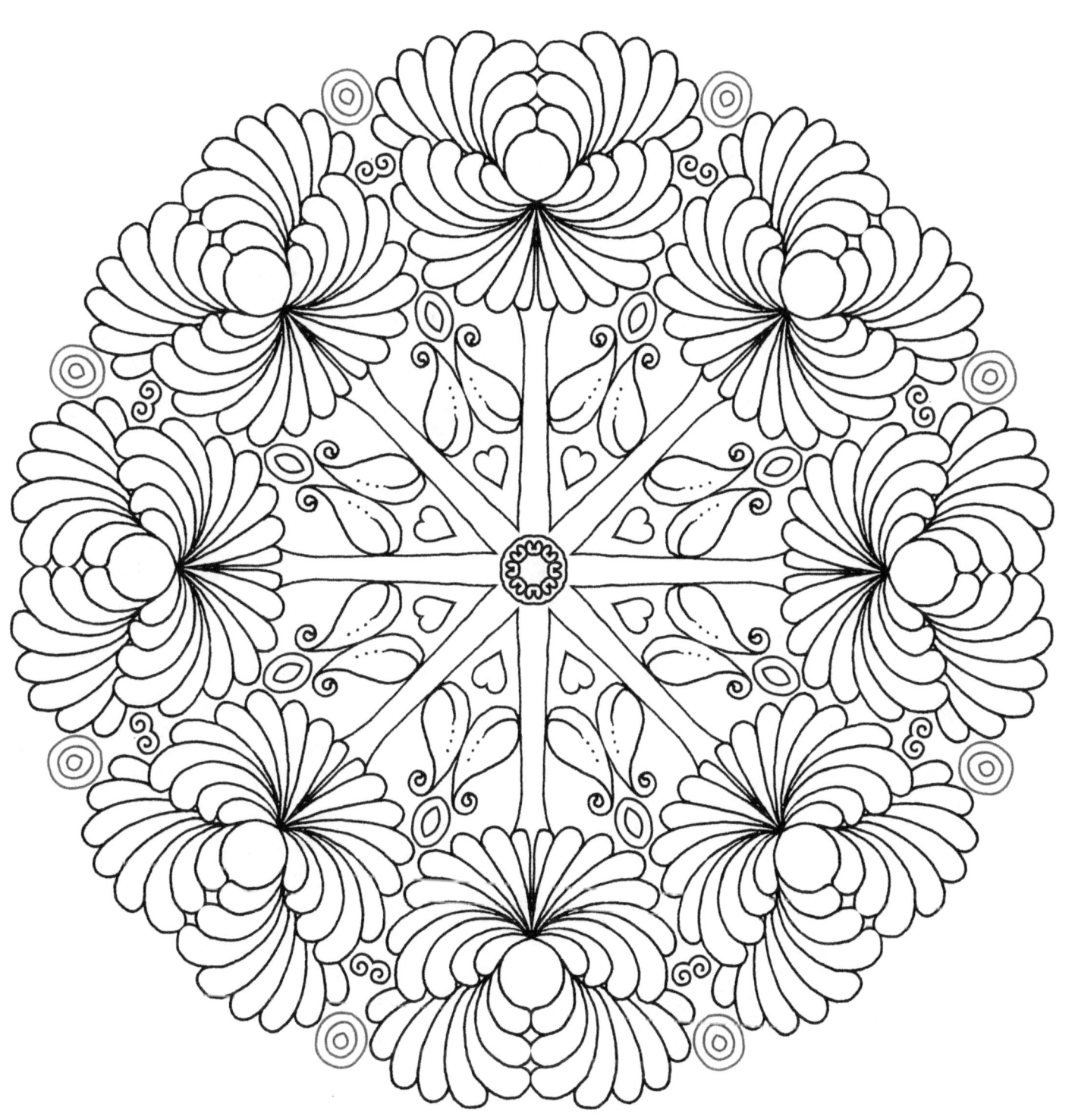

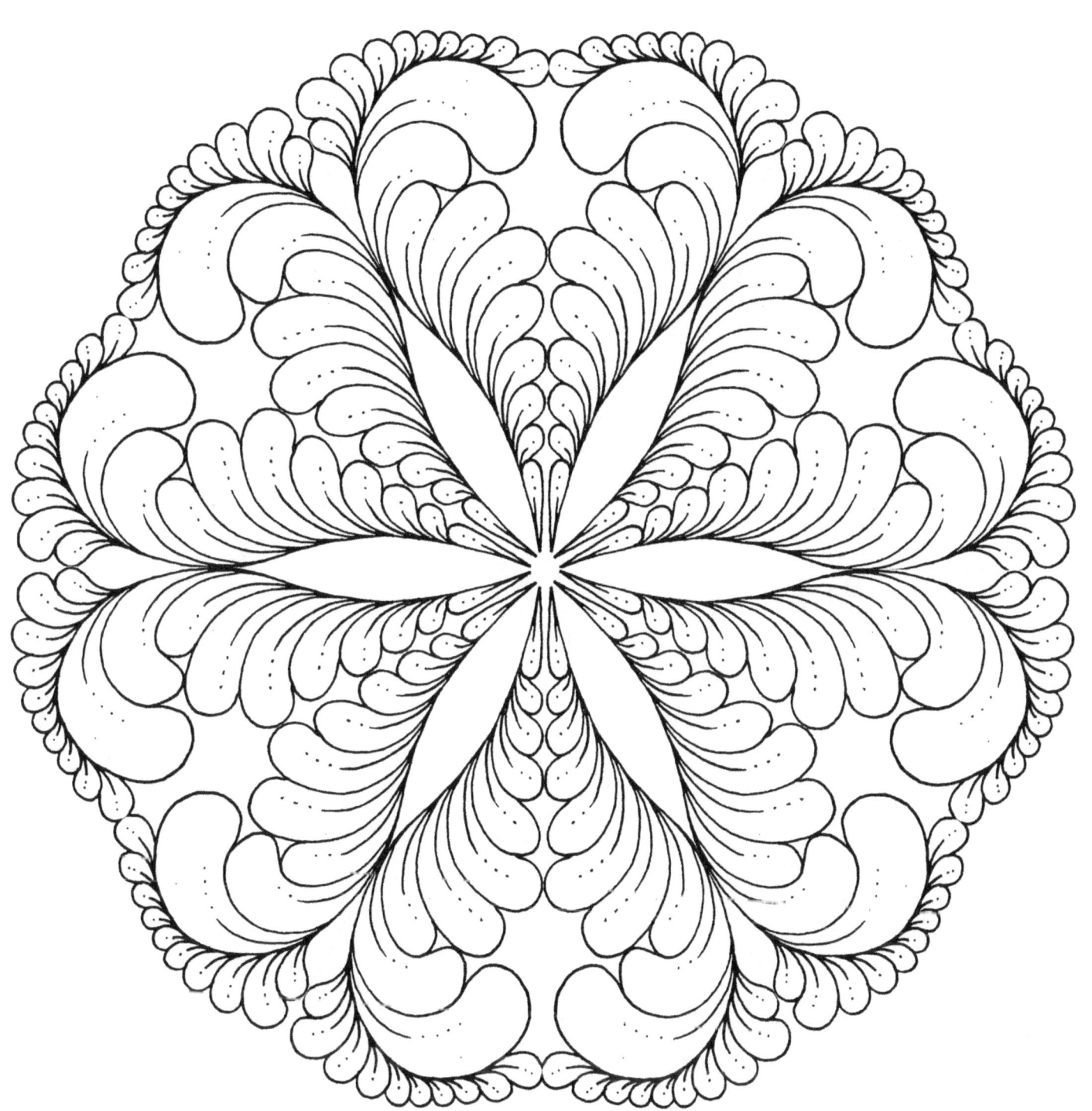

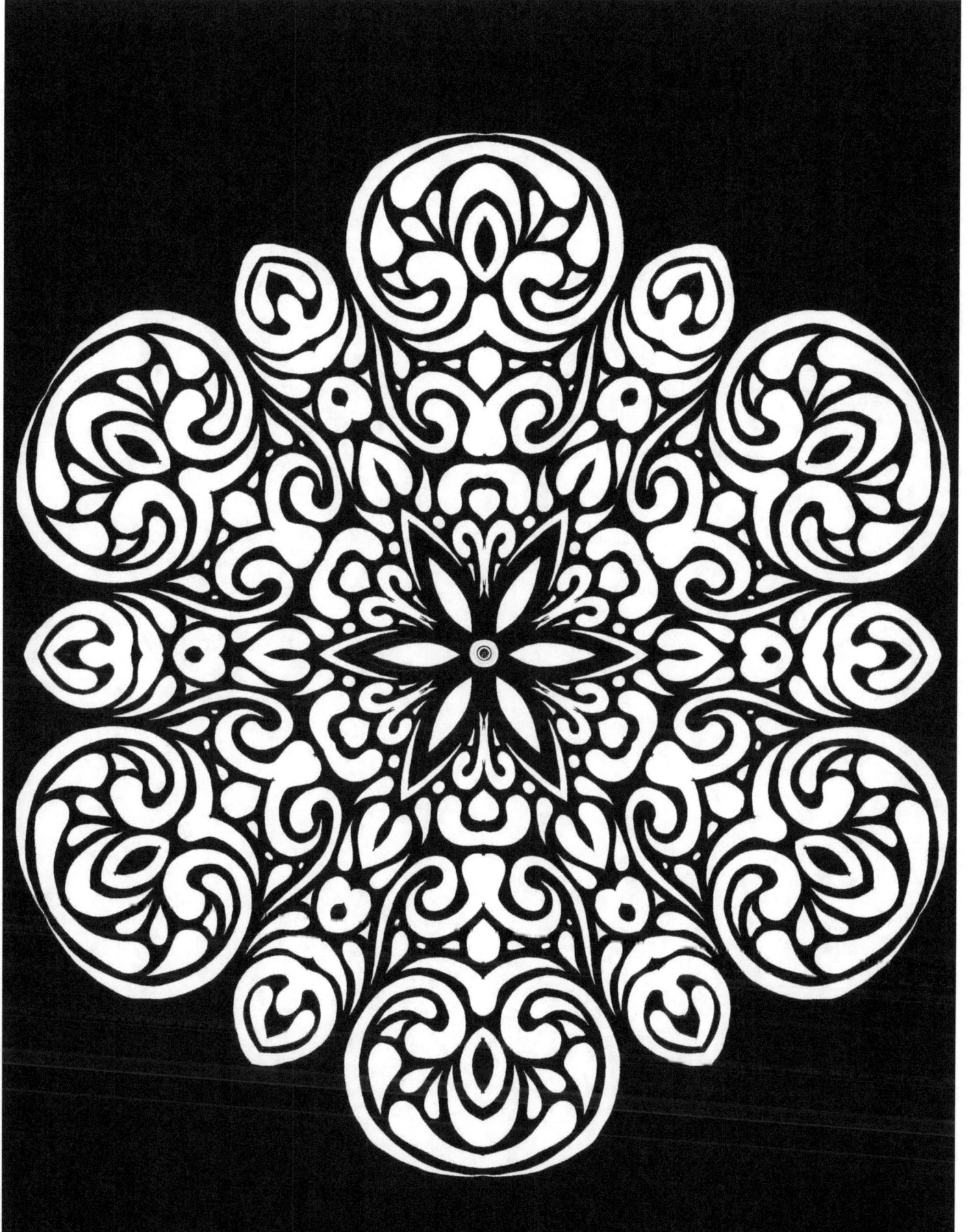

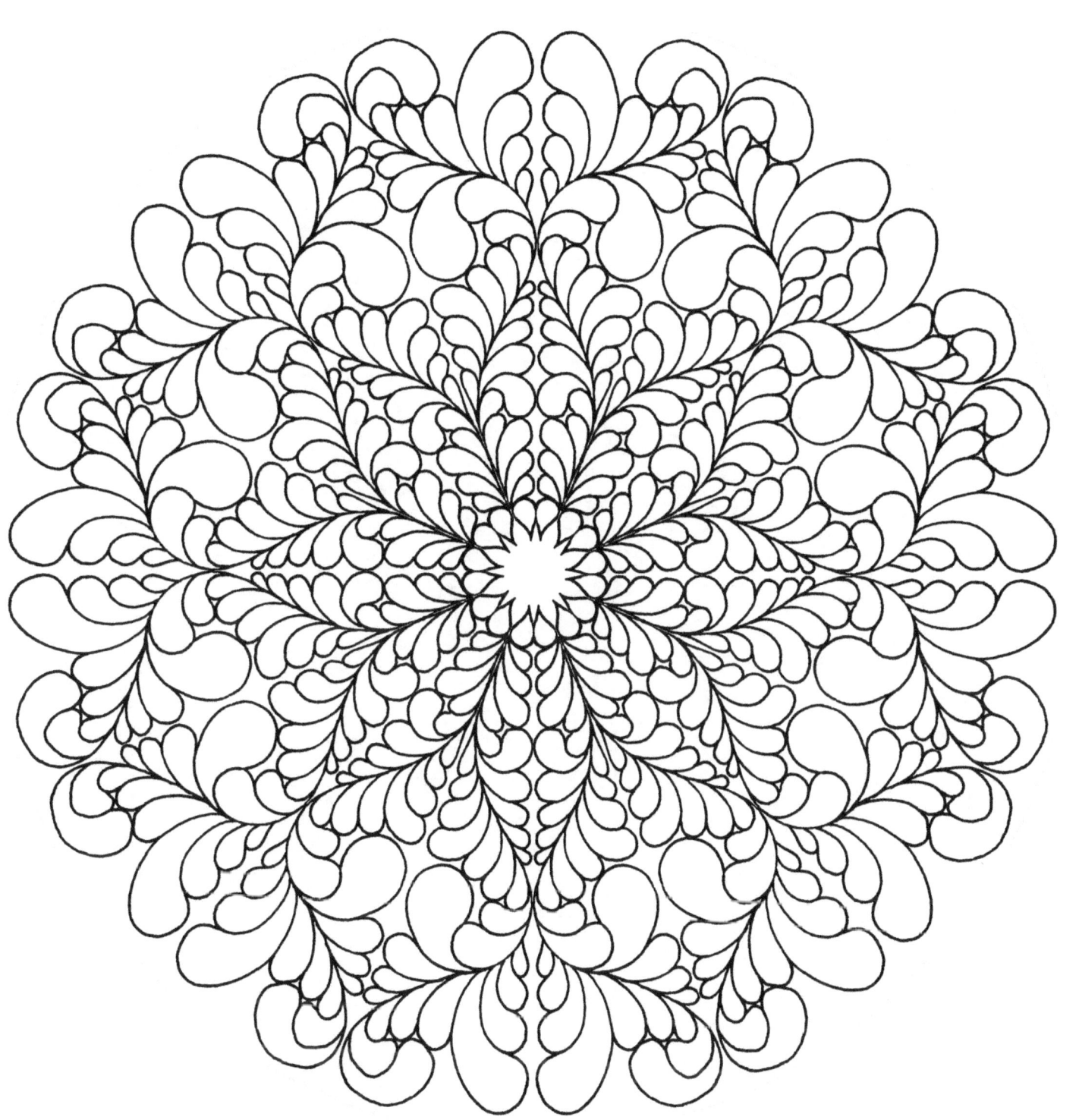

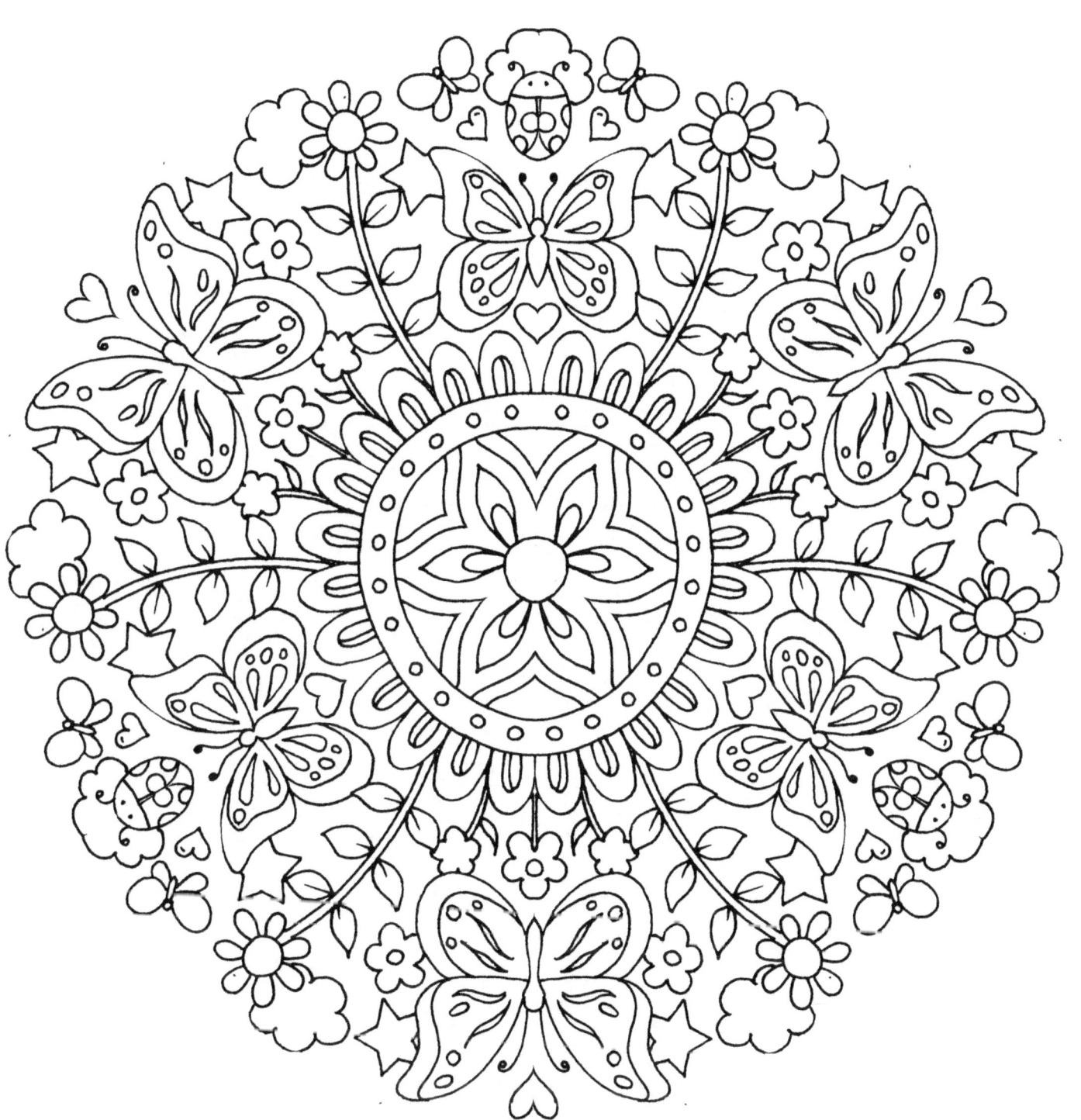

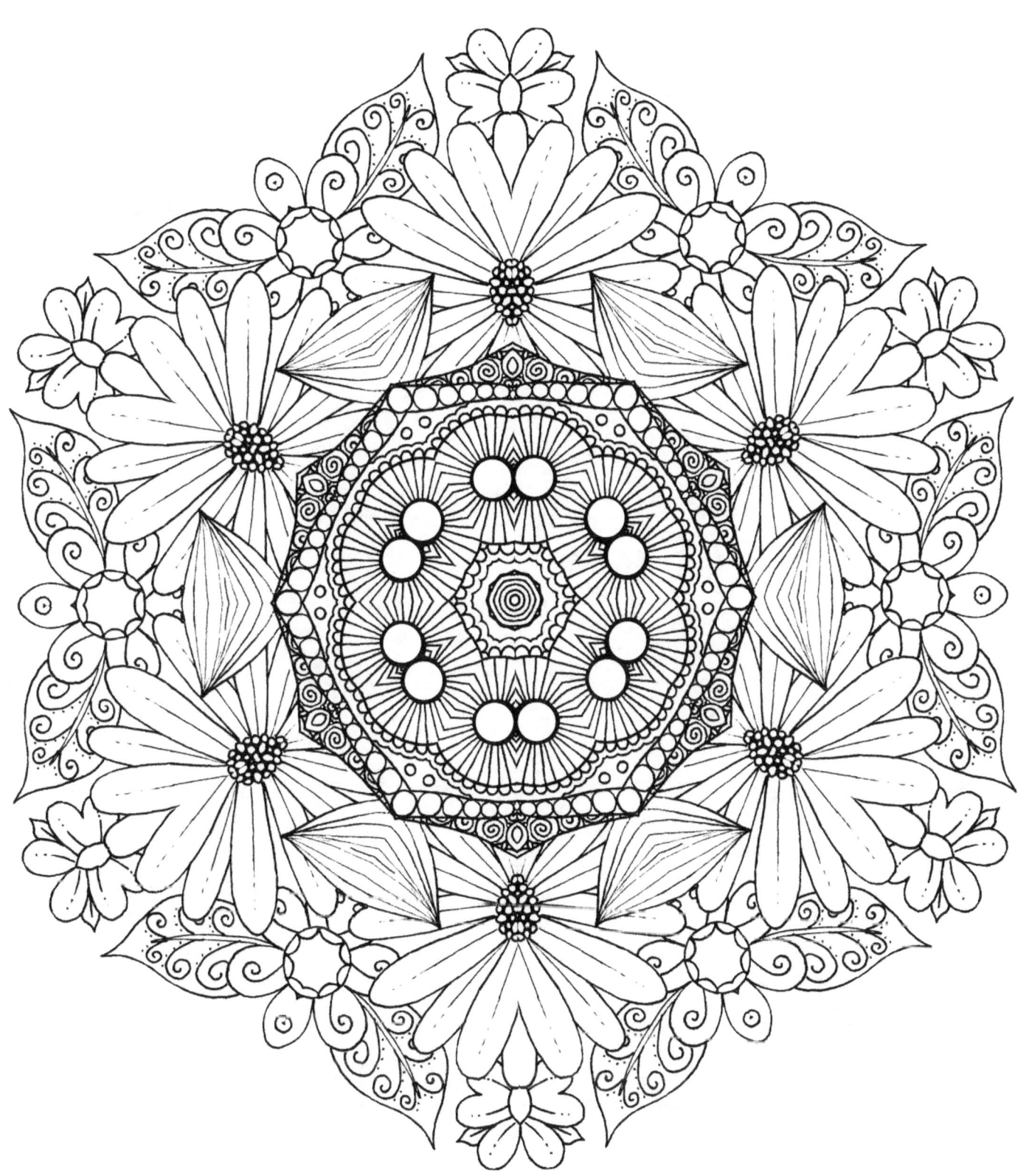

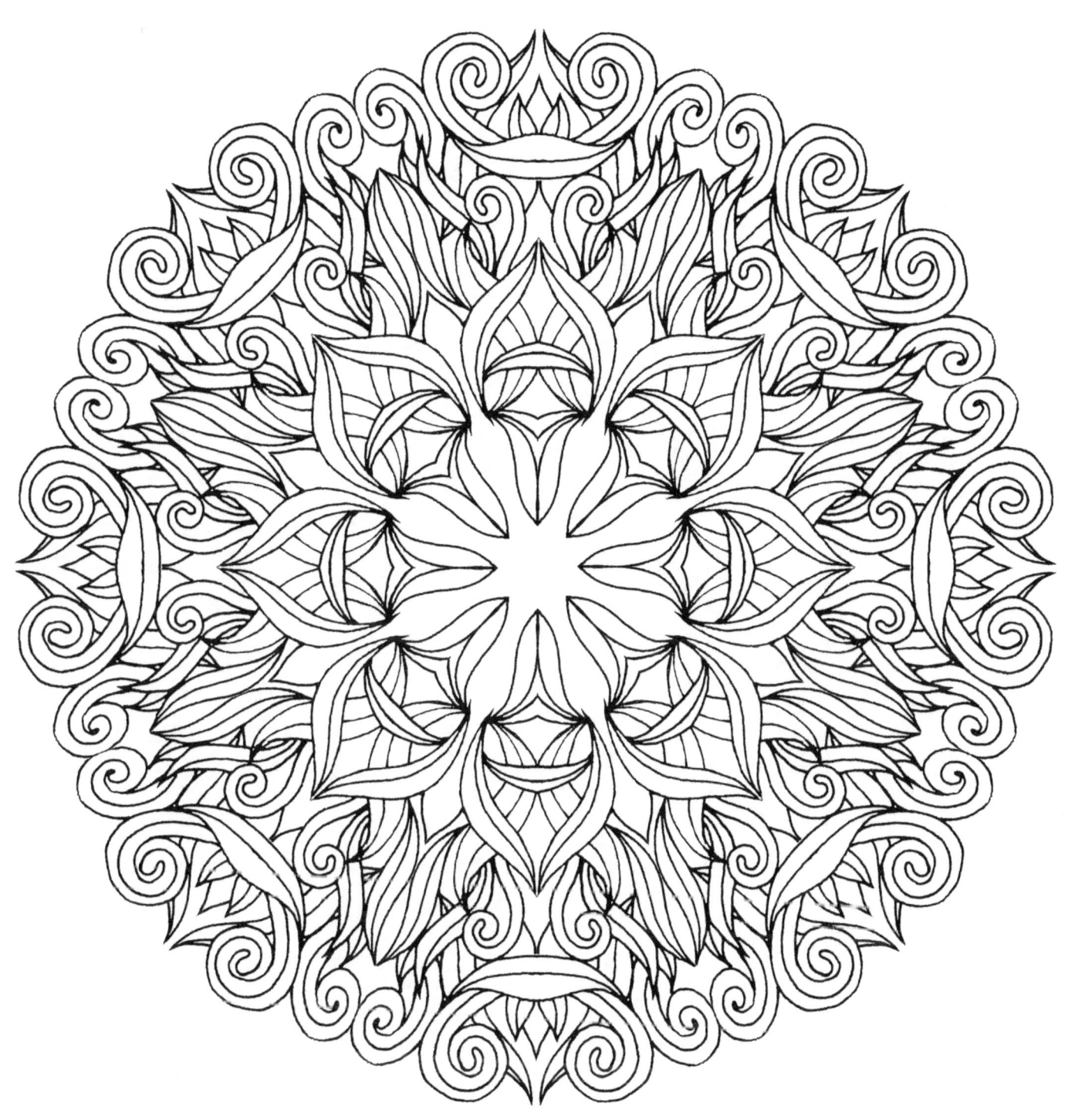

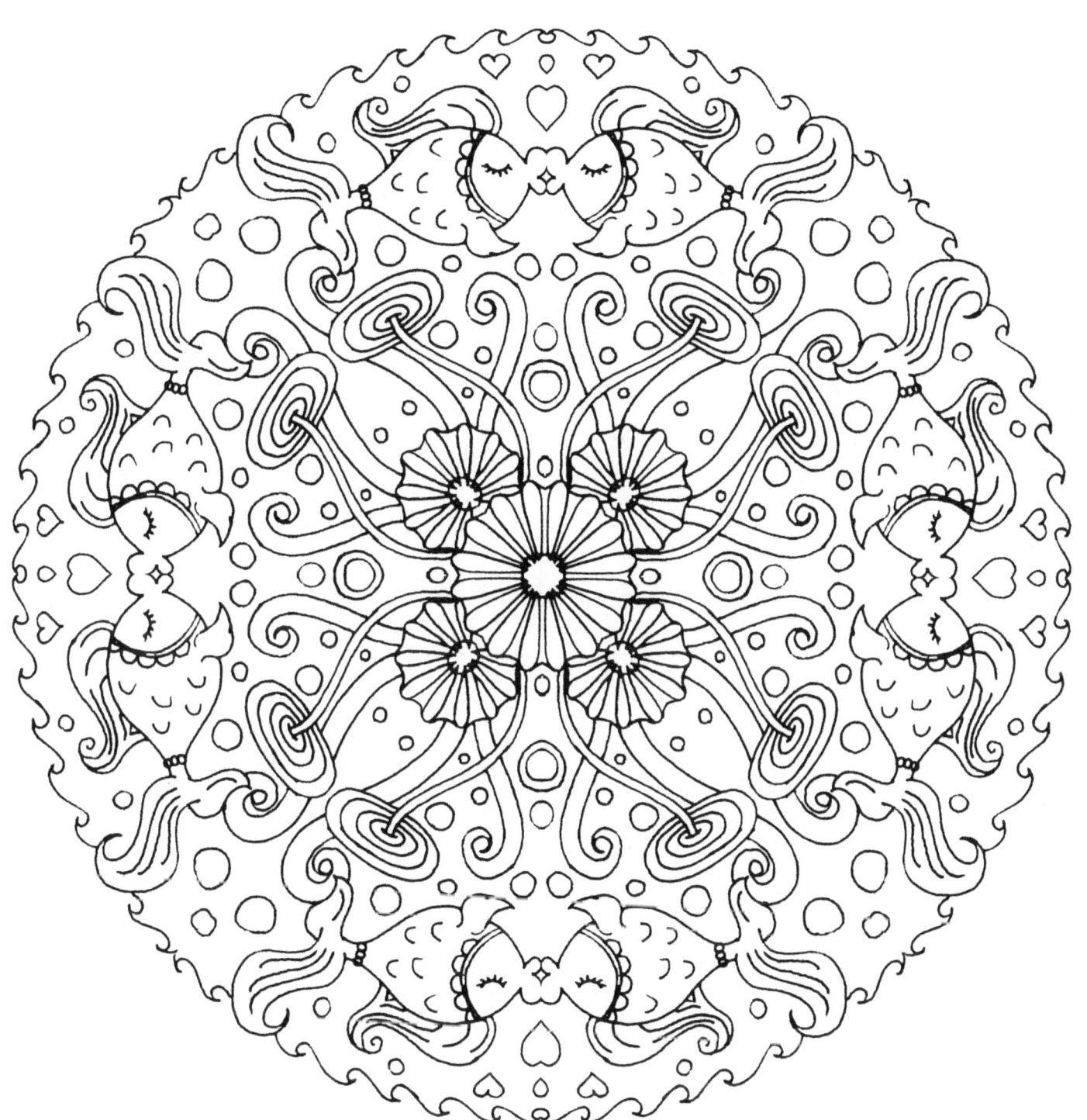

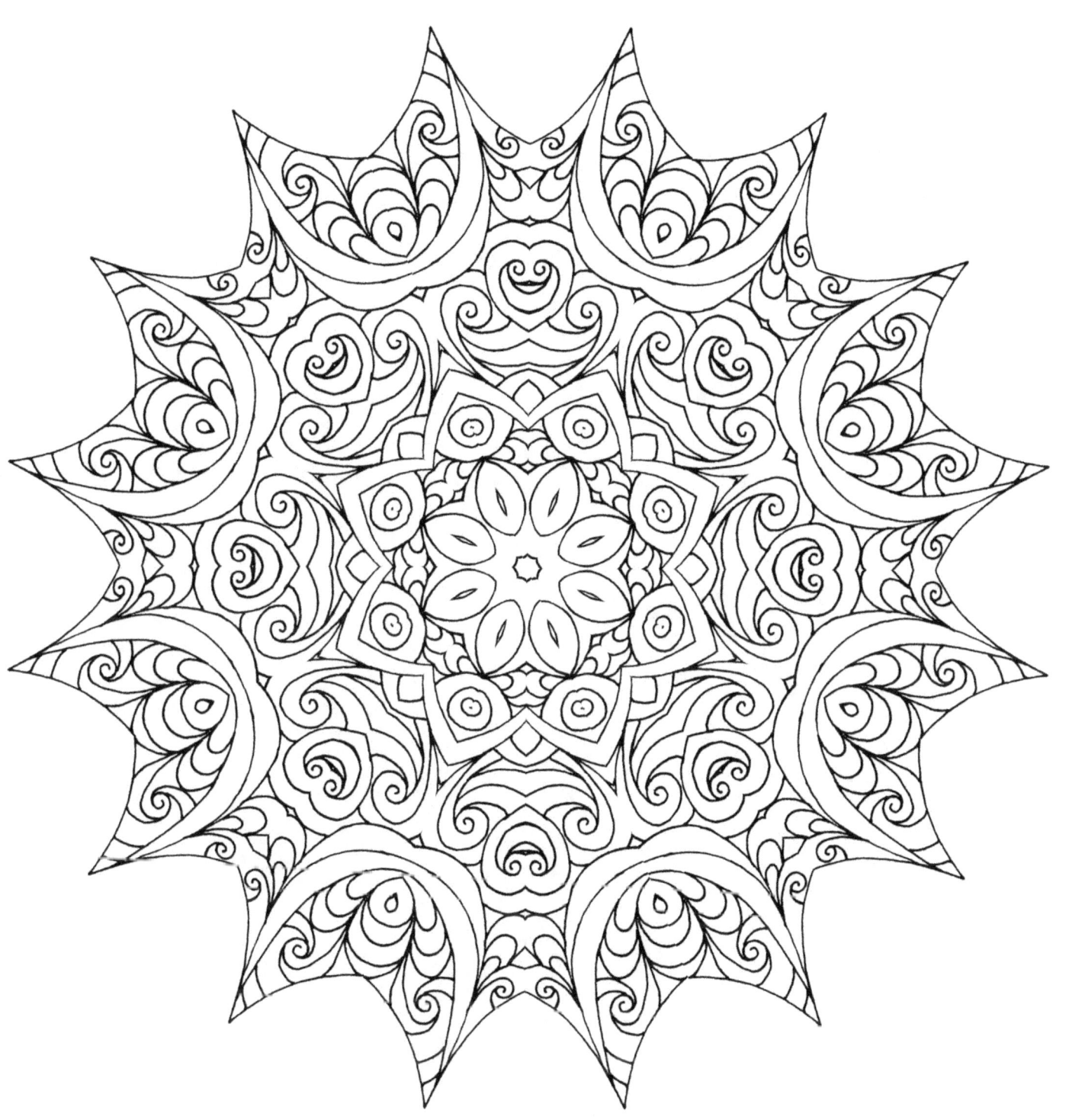

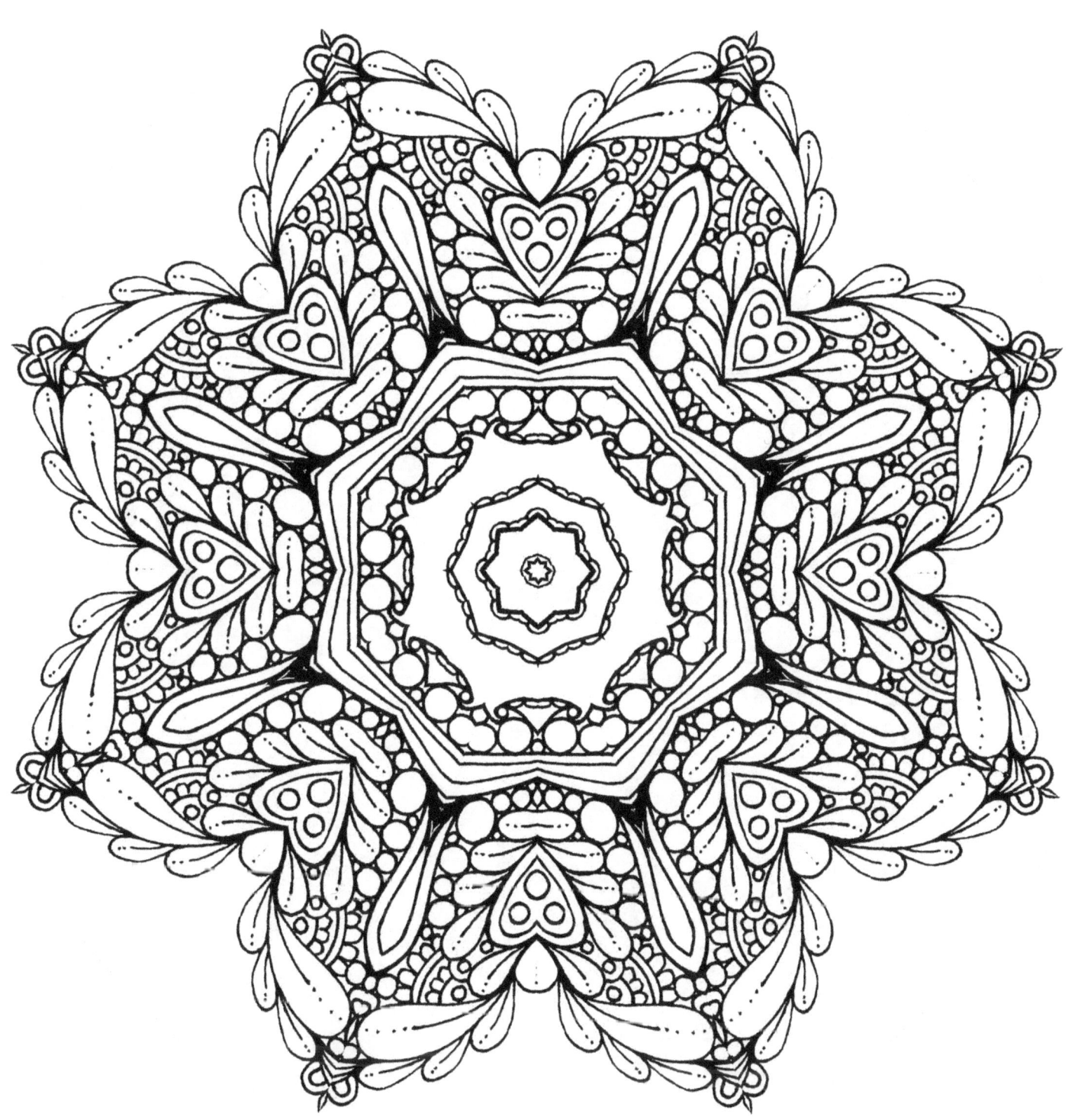

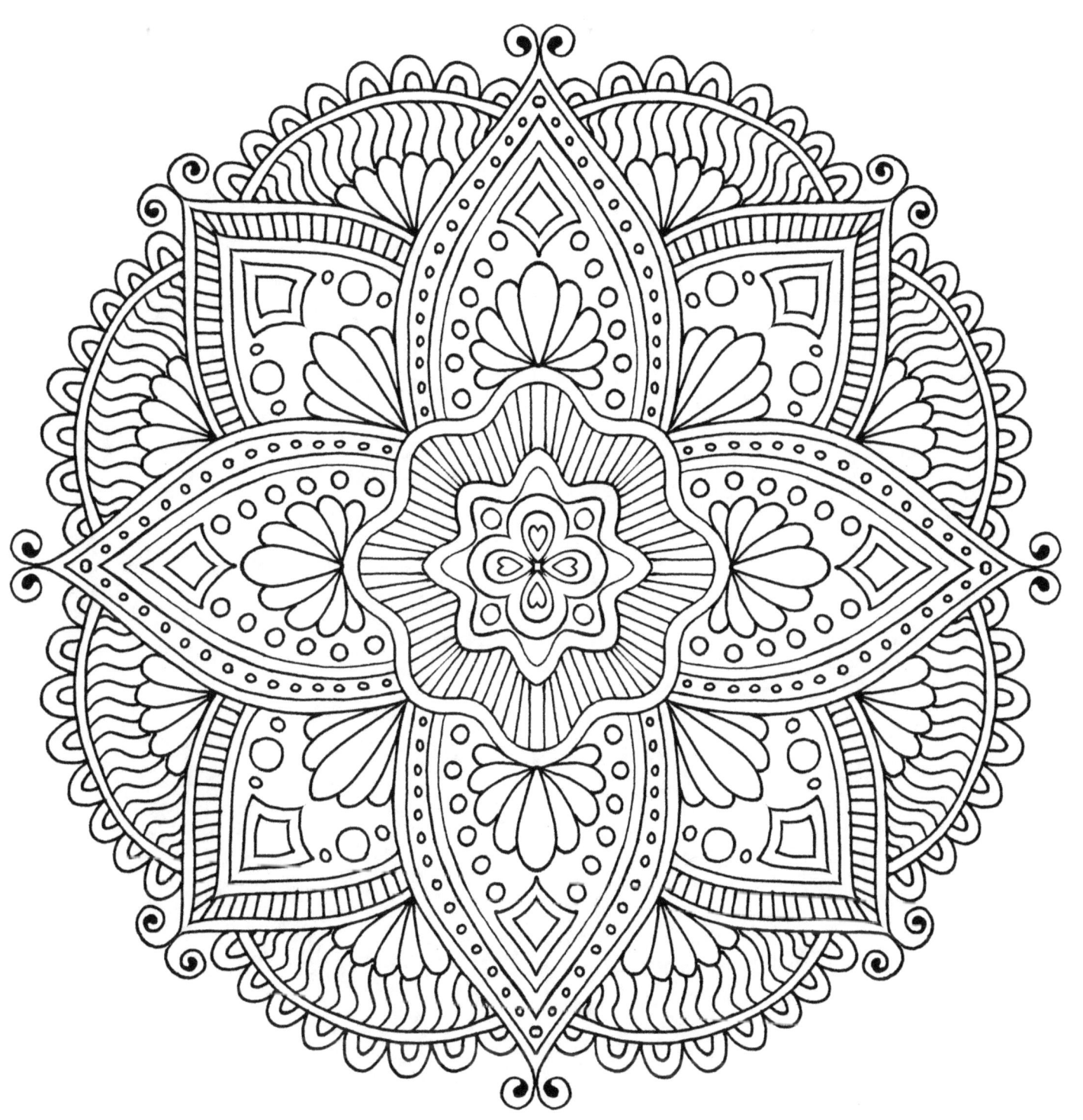

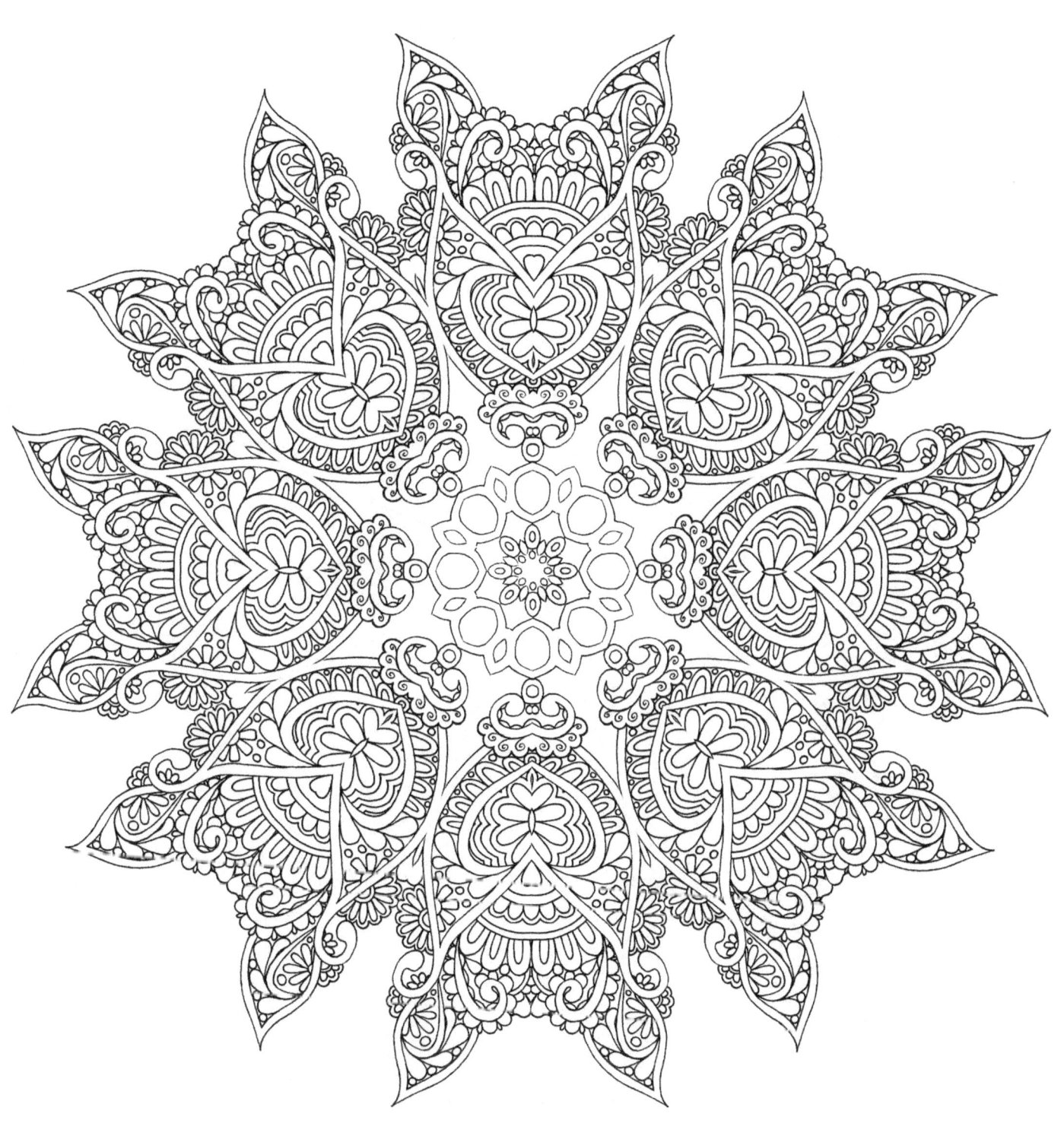

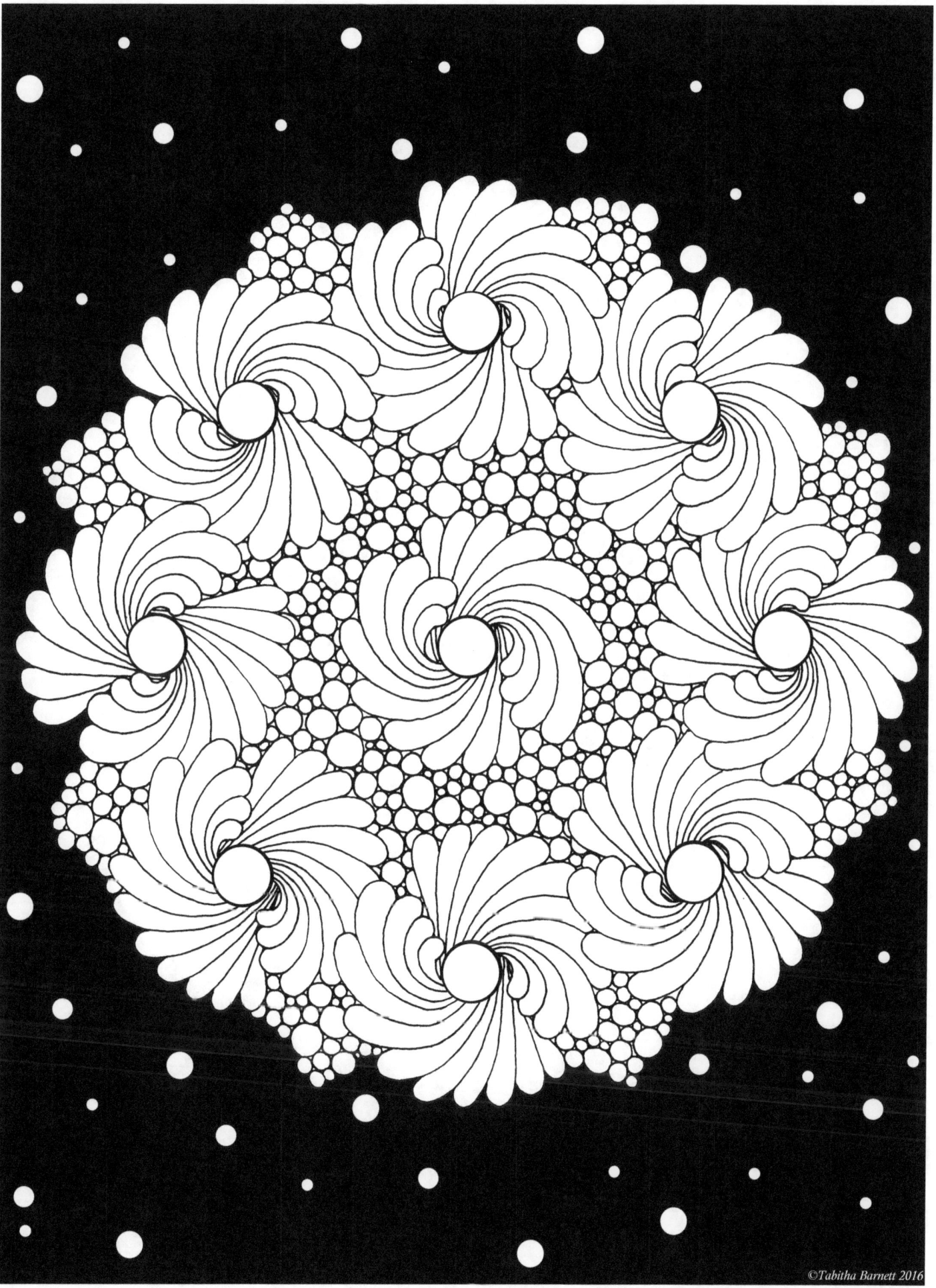

©Tabitha Barnett 2016

Thank you for purchasing "Majestic Mandalas Volume 1"! I hope you are thoroughly enjoying this book. I was VERY nervous about publishing a mandala book. There are so many already in publication. After posting some free mandalas on Facebook, I decided to go for it. Please visit me on the web and let me know what you think of my artwork!
Paperbacks on Amazon: www.amazon.com/author/tabbystangledart
Printable PDFs and single coloring pages: www.sellfy.com/tabbyb
www.facebook.com/tabbystangledart (I can always use more "likes")
twitter: @tabbyleann
Pinterest: tabbystangled art
www.facebook.com/tabby.barnett (Feel free to friend me, I'm always posting freebies!)
Patrons always welcome: www.patreon.com/tabbyb
Some pretty cool colorable merchandise: www.redbubble.com/people/tabbyb

If you enjoyed these mandalas...Volume 2 will be available soon! I am also working on a black background version of both books! I hope you'll enjoy this bonus butterfly from a future book.

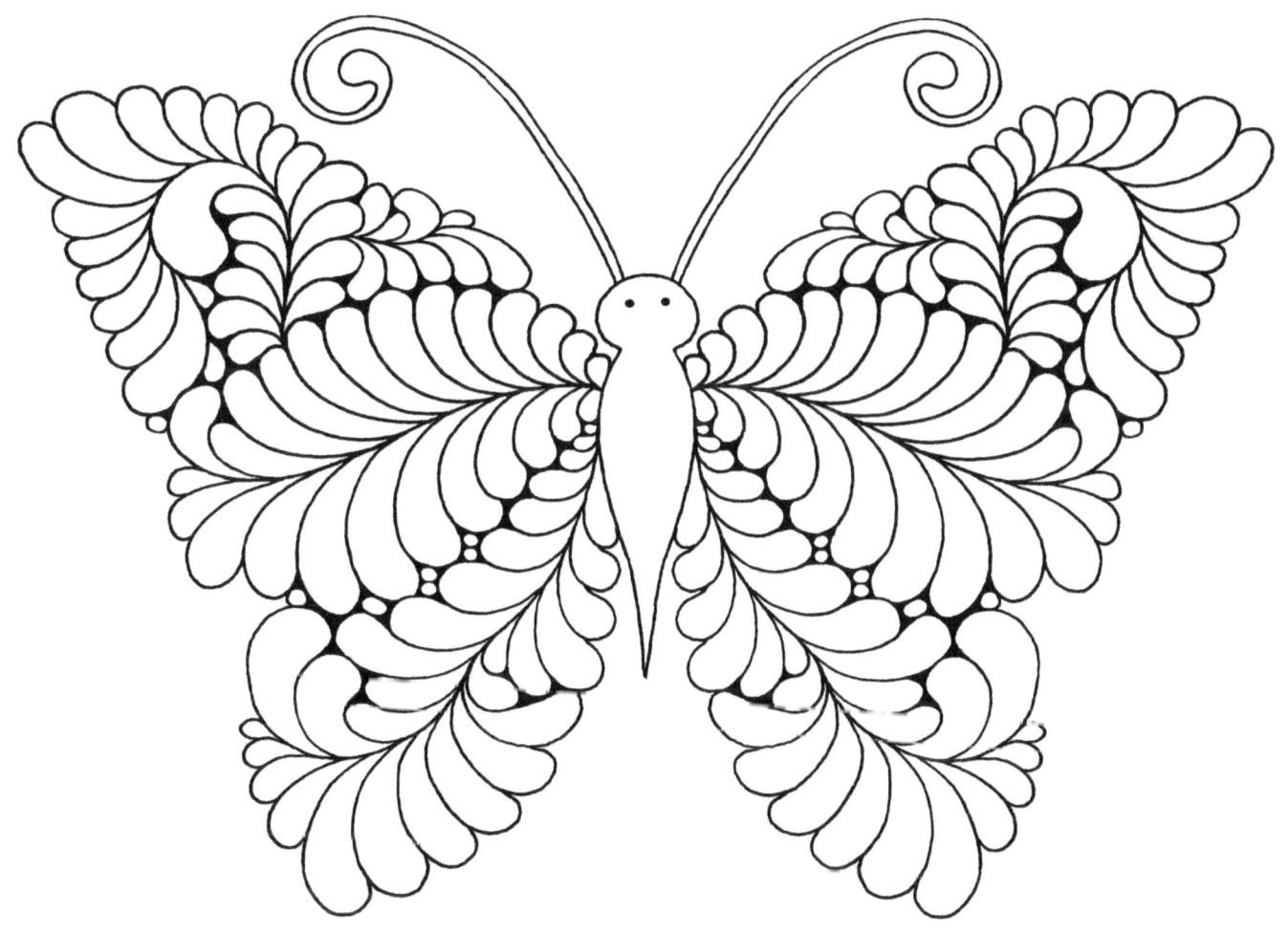

Favorite Color Blends